"*The Preeminent Jesus in My Father, My Pastor* is a call to make Jesus first in the home and in the church, in principle and in practice, in word and in deed. Dr. Timothy Dresselhaus had a front-row seat to watch in living color as his father, Dr. Richard Dresselhaus, modeled these truths before his family and his congregation. This book is not just a biography of a man but a reflection upon the greatness of Jesus made preeminent in the life of a father and the ministry of a pastor."

DOUG CLAY
General Superintendent, Assemblies of God
Springfield, Missouri

"In the winter of 1974, the economic downturn forced our touring music ministry to close. Master Design had just completed a new recording project with Light Records, making the closure even more painful. At the time, we lived in San Diego and had made First Assembly of God our spiritual home and Pastor Richard Dresselhaus our pastor. Out of work, Pastor Dresselhaus took pity on us and put me on pastoral staff in what would now be called an Executive Pastor role. The church had grown under his leadership and incredible teaching ministry, placing us in the middle of a huge building program. What an amazing learning curve! During these peak years of the Jesus Movement, it was not uncommon to see surfboards leaning against the walls of the lobby while young believers worshiped and hungered for the pure Word of God. For the next seven years, Pastor Dresselhaus mentored me, taught me, encouraged me, and allowed me to step into ministry roles in a thriving church. His exegetical preaching taught me to treat the Word of God as a sacred text carrying the power of the Holy Spirit to change lives. His rigorous personal faith disciplines taught me not to be sloppy but instead prayerful and thoughtful in my leadership. During this time, I watched, somewhat in disbelief, as a small contingent in the church tried to force him out. My disbelief was that he never once publicly defended himself. He told me that the Lord had said to him, 'You can defend yourself, and you have ample ammunition to do that. Or you can let Me defend you.' He said to me, 'Alec, I decided right then that I would rather have Him defend me.' And He did! I would sum up the life of Richard Dresselhaus with adjectives sadly not always associated with a pastor but descriptive through all the years I have known him: humble, understated, gracious, kind, quick to forgive, integrous, faithful, resilient, tenacious, and good! I am honored, after all these years, to still call him my friend!"

ALEC ROWLANDS, DMIN
Senior Pastor, Westgate Chapel
Seattle, Washington
Founder & President, Church Awakening

"The stated premise of *The Preeminent Jesus in my Father, My Pastor* underscores that public character must be grounded in private character to be credible. When the two are in contradiction, the result is cynicism and distrust by the segment of society being served. We live in an era of general distrust in leaders of all institutions. Clergy do not escape this trend. The value of this volume is as a vigilant reminder that there are human examples of leadership integrity worth emulating. More importantly, the premise of this volume is given visibility in a very specific human example: Pastor Richard Dresselhaus, whom I have had the privilege to call a friend for over fifty years. He is the classic 'what you see is what you get' man. As a young pastoral leader, I began my ministry with someone who believed in me, encouraged me, and with whom I could discuss the vast mysteries of ministry in the church. He has walked with me through my entire ministry. He was on the board of the seminary that hired me as its president, we worked together as colleagues, but he was always the elder brother. That his son would write this volume is telling. Tim knows his father well, in ways that few people will ever know him. That this volume would essentially be a theological reflection by a son using his father as a human example is profound. I have sometimes wondered about the Apostle Paul's injunction in 1 Corinthians 11:1, 'Be imitators of me, as I am of Christ.' But I have been privileged to know another man of God in my lifetime for whom this injunction makes perfect sense."

BYRON KLAUS, DMIN
Past President, Assemblies of God Theological Seminary
Oregon City, Oregon

"Haddon Robinson, a proponent of expository preaching, once said, 'There are no great sermons; there's only a great text. There are no great preachers; there's only a Great Christ!' Richard Dresselhaus, a proponent of expository preaching, modeled this distinction in the pulpit and in the home, and this is why I love the essence of *The Preeminent Jesus in My Father, My Pastor*. Three decades ago, when I started my journey as a local church pastor, Richard Dressehaus was in his prime as a lead pastor with international influence. I was a young pastor, and he befriended me, treating me as a peer. Consequently, his example inspired many of my early choices. Some years later, his son became my friend, and the more I grew to love Timothy, the more I loved his father. So, here you go. What's not to love about a book about a dad who loves Jesus and loves his son, written by his son who loves Jesus and loves his dad—especially when the dad wants the book his son is writing about him to be primarily about a Great Christ!"

DOUG GREEN, DMIN
Senior Pastor, North Hills Church
Brea, California

"In *The Preeminent Jesus in My Father, My Pastor*, the essence of Christ's teachings is heartfelt and revealed within the dual roles of home and church leadership. Timothy Dresselhaus captures the compelling exploration of the Christlike virtues that should anchor our lives, both in quiet moments with family and in guiding a flock. It honors not the man, Richard Dresselhaus, but the reflection of Christ within him—a mirror of godliness we should all strive to polish in our daily lives. Few men have had a more significant influence on my life and ministry than the presence of Christ in Richard Dresselhaus."

TONY FOGLIO, DDIV
Founder & Pastor Emeritus, Sonrise Church
Santee, California

"*The Preeminent Jesus in My Father, My Pastor* is a wonderful mix of biblical commentary, vignettes from church history, personal stories, and Christian apologetics. It immerses the reader into Paul's theology, particularly his exaltation of Jesus as the all-powerful and preeminent Savior and Lord in Colossians 1 and describes the faithful expression of these truths in the life of the author's father and pastor, Richard Dresselhaus. The result is a biblically faithful, spiritually edifying, and intellectually engaging account of a father's impact on his son, enabled by the reconciling work of the Father through the Son, 'who is the image of the invisible God' (Colossians 1:15)."

ROBERT MENZIES, PHD
Director, Asian Center for Pentecostal Theology
Author of *Christ-Centered*
Springfield, Missouri

"*The Preeminent Jesus in My Father, My Pastor* echoes across more than 45 years since I was a new believer being discipled by the teaching and example of Pastor Richard Dresselhaus. Through the integration of his lifetime of personal observations and the thoughtful examination of biblical foundations and theological convictions, Dr. Timothy Dresselhaus reflects on the life-message of his father and a critical challenge for Christians today: keeping Christ preeminent in the home and in the church. This is essential reading for believers on both sides of the pulpit. It is a call to mobilize confession into action and a glimpse of the influence of a father on the faith of his son."

MICHAEL BEALS, PHD
President, Vanguard University
Costa Mesa, California

"Dr. Timothy Dresselhaus has written an incredible book that not only honors his father and his pastor, Dr. Richard Dresselhaus, but also conveys tremendous truths concerning the preeminent Jesus in his incarnation, creation, church, resurrection, cross, and mercy. *The Preeminent Jesus in My Father, My Pastor* expresses theological truths that spoke to my spirit, prompting emotions of gratitude for the amazing grace of Jesus. I will read this book many more times as it addresses the most important goals that I hold as I desire to display the preeminent Jesus in all that I do. Pastor Richard Dresselhaus was my wife, Rosalyn's, pastor, and he performed our wedding shortly after the start of his tenure in San Diego. He became pastor to both of us then and, as we have since served in many ministry endeavors, has remained our pastor at a distance for more than fifty years."

WAYDE GOODALL, DMIN
President, The Goodall Group
Colorado Springs, Colorado

THE PREEMINENT JESUS
IN
MY FATHER, MY PASTOR

Making Christ First at Home and at Church

Timothy Richard Dresselhaus

Copyright © 2024 by Timothy R. Dresselhaus, MD, MPH
ALL RIGHTS RESERVED

Cover design by Lauren Short

No portion of this book may be reproduced, stored in a retrieval system, or transmitted in any form or by any means—electronic, mechanical, photocopy, recording, or any other—except for brief quotations in printed reviews, without the prior written permission of the publisher. Write: Permissions, ACPT Press, P.O. Box 11032, Springfield, MO 65808, USA or email: ThePreeminentJesus@gmail.com.

Scripture quotations are from the ESV® Bible (The Holy Bible, English Standard Version®), copyright © 2001 by Crossway, a publishing ministry of Good News Publishers. Used by permission. All rights reserved.

Hardback ISBN: 979-8-9873845-4-1
Paperback ISBN: 979-8-9873845-2-7
eBook ISBN: 979-8-9873845-3-4

Library of Congress Control Number: 2023922537

To my father, my pastor—Richard Dresselhaus—who made Jesus preeminent in our home and in our church, setting a worthy and lasting example for his family and his congregation.

Table of Contents

Foreword	13
Introduction	21
Chapter 1: Preeminent in His Incarnation	27
Chapter 2: Preeminent in His Creation	39
Chapter 3: Preeminent in His Church	53
Chapter 4: Preeminent in His Resurrection	69
Chapter 5: Preeminent in His Cross	81
Chapter 6: Preeminent in His Mercy	93
Chapter 7: Preeminent in His Word	105
Afterword: The Priority of Example	117
Epilogue	121
Questions for Reflection and Discussion	125
Acknowledgments	131
About the Author	133

FOREWORD

As I sat down to write this Foreword, I felt a strong urging to first spend some time in God's Word, followed by a time of prayer. I wanted to be sure that what I wrote was first and foremost honoring to the Lord and, secondly, honoring to the father and pastor to whom this book is dedicated.

As I finished praying, got out my yellow pad, and began to consider what I might write, a smile came across my face as I realized that I was participating in the very point of this wonderful book authored by Timothy Dresselhaus.

Why had I first felt so strongly compelled to seek the Lord before I sought out the memories logged in the library of my mind and the experiences of my life's journey? The answer is quite simple. As a young Christian I had been taught carefully and consistently, "Put Jesus first and always keep Him first!"

Who had taught me this most important and essential truth? Godly parents, grandparents, and other redeemed family and friends had articulated and displayed the importance and absolute necessity of the "Jesus first" paradigm. However, I believe the one who clearly established this as a cornerstone in the foundation of my life was Dick.

If you know of whom I am speaking (and many of you do), you may think it somewhat disrespectful referring to Dr. Richard Dresselhaus, Reverend Dresselhaus, or Pastor Dresselhaus as simply … Dick. That is how he first introduced himself to me when I was a teenager, and it just stuck. If you do not know this man of God, you will come to know him in the following pages. More importantly, you are about to be introduced, or perhaps reintroduced, to the preeminent Jesus who was, is, and forever shall be the central focus of Dick's life and ministry.

In 1961, our parents announced to my brother and me that we were going to visit a new church about ten miles from our house. We had grown up in a little church in St. Paul Park, Minnesota. It was exactly one and a half blocks from our house. Many family members and friends also attended that church. "Why the need to visit somewhere else," I wondered? Were we just going to visit or were our parents thinking of switching to another church?

I had just turned thirteen and was now old enough to participate in the youth group in our little fellowship. A thirteen-year-old girl from a sister church in our denomination had caught my eye at a combined youth event, and I thought it might be nice to get to know her. When our parents announced to my brother and me that they were thinking of attending this new church on a regular basis, I thought to myself, "This is not good timing!"

I think mom and dad sensed that I was quite resistant to the idea, so they came up with a plan that would give me a way to "opt out" if I should so choose. Their offer was as follows: "Come with us to Summit Avenue Assembly of God just three Sundays in a row, and then we will let you decide whether or not we will go or stay put." I thought to myself, "Hey, I can endure anything for just three Sundays, then my choice will seal our destiny and back to normal we will go."

The first Sunday we set off to visit Summit Avenue I was almost sick from being so nervous. I was a very shy young man and the thought of walking into a Sunday School class of boys my age, whom I did not know, was intimidating, to say the least. At the end of class, I met Norm, Bob, Tim, Dave, Allen, and Jim. They asked where I lived and befriended me, at least to the extent of their teenage capabilities.

Then we moved into the main sanctuary for the morning worship service. After some preliminaries, the song service started. First, they had a band along with a pianist and organist, who were both excellent musicians. In the band was an upright bass, a couple of accordions, a tenor sax, some other instruments, and ... wait for it ... an electric guitar!

The congregation sang passionately and loudly! They sang songs like "Victory in Jesus" and "What a Friend We Have in Jesus." Many congregants clapped along with the rhythm of the songs. Some people raised their hands as they sang. I had never witnessed anything like this in church. Passion and volume did not describe the music at the little church we grew up in. I am pretty sure clapping during a song would have solicited a caution from an usher. And raising a hand was a permissible gesture during a church business meeting but not recommended behavior during worship.

The service at Summit continued after the singing with the preaching of the Word. Pastor Wilbur Weides, a kind, compassionate, and godly man, brought forth the message from the text of scripture, with the confidence and authority that only one who had spent time on his knees and in the Word would be able to do. After the service, Pastor Weides introduced himself to me and seemed genuinely interested in meeting a thirteen-year-old visitor.

And then I met Dick. He simply extended his hand and said, "Hi, I'm Dick, what's your name?" He had been on the platform during the service, and I think he had announced the youth group service. I really had not paid much attention because, after all, in another two weeks I would be out of there!

Dick was a kind, gracious, and seemingly intentional young adult who had the most perfectly squared off red-haired crew cut I had ever seen! I think his position at the church was sort of assistant pastor/youth director. I am not sure if that was his actual title or not. It seemed to me that described his responsibilities. I would come to know him better in the ensuing months and years.

I wish I could continue with wonderful memories of that time in my life at Summit Avenue Assembly, with those saints of God, many, if not most, who have gone on to be with Jesus. Time and space do not permit.

However, there are two important events in my life, perhaps the most important, that I would like to share, both involving Dick's ministry and impact upon my life and ministry.

As you may have guessed, by the third week of attending Summit Avenue, I had decided that I would be okay attending there regularly. I think the music won me over more than anything, but there was also a freedom, liberty, and joy present in that church that I had not heretofore experienced.

Though I was raised in a Christian home and had attended church on a regular basis, I had not yet surrendered my life to Jesus. I believed the Bible to be true. I knew who Jesus was and what he had done, but I was not ready or willing to admit my need of a Savior.

Quite frankly, I was having a good time, enjoying my life, and pursuing my musical quest to be a rock star. My brother and I both played guitar and had played some in high school rock bands. When he moved on to other interests, I pursued it a little more aggressively, playing more and more at parties, dances, and clubs on the weekends. I was quite young to be pursuing this dream as passionately as I was, but all I did was eat, sleep and dream rock and roll.

Then one Sunday night, on October 17, 1965, my brother and I were to contribute a musical piece during the Sunday evening service. Before the service began, Dick—who had now become the senior pastor at Summit Avenue—asked my brother and me if he could have a moment with us before the service. We went down into a little church office in the basement, and, with the same kindness and intentionality that he had always displayed, he simply shared his concern about the spiritual condition of our lives. My brother had recently come back into right relationship with the Lord, so that left the finger pointing at me.

Unbeknownst to me, Dick had been made aware of my "rock career" and thus his concern about my participation in a church worship time. I "beat around the bush" a little in response to Dick's question and concern about my soul, but he lovingly continued to press the issue. All I can say is that because of his concern and obedience, and God's loving conviction, I surrendered my life to Jesus right then and there. Best moment ever!

I remember shortly thereafter thinking, "If I'm going to live for Jesus, then I'm going to sing for Jesus and for him only." Thus, my ministry began. Almost immediately, opportunities for ministry began for me. Suddenly, I was going out most weekends, singing and sharing my testimony somewhere.

One Sunday morning while back at Summit Avenue, I was making my way toward the front of the building over on the side aisle as Dick was making his way toward the back. As we met, he asked, "Dallas, could I share something with you?" Always appreciating his input and his wisdom, I said, "Absolutely." What followed may be the single most important piece of advice I have ever received. He said, "Dallas, you're going to have all your life to minister but you're only going to have one chance to prepare, and that's now. Let me encourage you during this season to stay home, here in this church. Let me teach you, let me disciple you, and build a foundation upon God's Word beneath your life and ministry. Go out every few weeks to develop the way in which you'll minister, but for the greater part, stay home ... build the foundation!"

I took his advice. I stayed home, and together by God's grace, upon His Word, and upon an understanding of the preeminence of Christ in my life and calling, we built a foundation that has never failed in over a half century of ministry! I have failed at times as have all of us, but the foundation remains sure, the ministry of the gospel continues, and my commitment to Christ is stronger than ever. Through songs, recordings, concerts, radio, and a host of other mediums and opportunities, I have had the privilege to present the gospel to literally millions of people around the world. All this because a pastor cared enough about a wayward teenager who just needed Jesus.

Thank you, Dick!

Dick led me to faith in Christ. He baptized me. He helped me build the foundation of my life and ministry. He married my wife Linda (a Summit Avenue girl) and me on December 27, 1969. We recently observed our fifty-fourth wedding anniversary, three days before Linda went to be with Jesus. Our wonderful marriage was built upon the same foundation of God's Word and the preeminence of Christ. Dick was one of the first to call and offer sympathy and prayerful support after Linda's passing.

Thank you, Dick!

Through the years as I have needed counsel and wisdom, I have called upon Dick because I knew I would receive biblical, prayerful, and wise counsel. What a blessing, what a friend!

I know you are anxious to read the book, so I will wrap up this Foreward. It is just that hindsight is so crystal clear. As a young man, my life seemed to stretch far out before me towards a seemingly unreachable horizon. Now, as an older man, the path that remains ahead is not so long. I can see the horizon. That which now lies behind is as a path stretching far back into the past; so distant is its beginning that some memories fade, so I want to remember and share the ones that hold such meaning for me.

I am pretty sure when Dick reads this, he will blush a little with embarrassment, desiring sincerely to direct all attention to our wonderful Savior. However, the Scripture, to which Dick so consistently points us all, does proclaim, "Give honor to whom honor is due" (Romans 13:7).

Lastly, thank you, Tim, for authoring this absolute treasure of sound theological substance, warm meaningful insights, and helpful practical applications. We have a saying, "He's a chip off the old block!" Your dad is not a block; he is a bulwark who has faithfully, patiently, and graciously withstood the assaults of the enemy and the test of time. You are not a chip; you are the very embodiment of your father's example and beliefs. You possess his DNA physically, intellectually, and spiritually, all to the glory of God (and your proud father's pleasure).

Thank you, Tim!

Through the years, by God's grace and kindness, I have been afforded many honors and awards. None rank higher in my estimation than the invitation to write this Foreword. May the Lord be glorified and may Pastor Richard Dresselhaus be honored.

Now, I will get out of the way and let the reader read *The Preeminent Jesus in My Father, My Pastor,* one of the most meaningful and uplifting books you are ever going to read!

DALLAS HOLM
Gospel Hall of Fame, Grammy Award-Nominated,
and Dove Award-Winning Artist
Lindale, Texas

INTRODUCTION

That in everything he might be preeminent.
Colossians 1:18

On a balmy Friday afternoon in December 2015, I stopped by my parent's home to retrieve several grocery items they had picked up for my family at Costco. Cash in hand, I offered to reimburse my father. "No," he said, "I don't have forever to be generous." Though eighty years old at the time, he enjoyed good health and had remained very active. Still, he was aware of his mortality and life's brevity. He later shifted the conversation from the current events we were discussing to a mid-week service at which I taught two nights prior. "Wednesday night after Bible study, I thought to ask you to be the main speaker at my memorial. *Make sure you don't talk about how great I was but how great Jesus is.*"

This request captures the attitude that has imbued my father's life in the home and my pastor's ministry in the church. In these twin roles, Richard Dresselhaus—my father, my pastor—has sought to make Jesus preeminent. In fact, his life verse, which will someday be etched on his grave marker, is drawn from Colossians 1:18: "That in everything he might be preeminent."

This commitment to the preeminence of Jesus appeared very early in his life and ministry. He first learned of its significance as a youth through the influence of his elder brother, Elton, who would give his life to missionary service in Venezuela. Later, in his first pastorate at Summit Avenue Assembly of God in St. Paul, Minnesota, a birthday reception in his honor was planned. My mom was asked to suggest an apt Bible verse with which to decorate the celebratory cake. Without hesitation, she suggested Colossians 3:18, in her mind remembering "that in everything he may be preeminent." Confusion ensued when the thoughtful planners read: "Wives, submit to your husbands, as is fitting in the Lord." While Colossians 3:18 may be meaningful to my father, it is not his life verse. Thankfully, the confusion was resolved and Colossians 1:18—not 3:18—adorned the birthday cake.

It is easy to claim that Jesus is preeminent; it is much more difficult to live in a manner that lines up with this timeless priority. My father sought to translate this noble principle into practice by giving Jesus the first place in our home and in our church. His many years of experience notwithstanding, I know he would consider "that in everything he might be preeminent" an aspiration that is still not fully realized. He would hold that the full realization of this truth is experienced not in time but in eternity, for "what we will be has not yet appeared; but we know that when he appears we shall be like him, because we shall see him as he is."[1]

Nonetheless, Paul's letter to the Colossians—intended to help a fledgling church remain faithful and true in the face of false teachings that depreciated the person of Christ—is an urgent call to make Jesus preeminent in the here and now. In a declaration that is both poetic and hymnic, Paul employs synonyms for Jesus' preeminence such as "the firstborn of all creation," "the firstborn from the dead," "the head," "by him all things," "before all things," and "the fullness of God":

> He is the image of the invisible God, the firstborn of all creation. For by him all things were created, in heaven and on earth, visible and invisible, whether thrones or dominions or rulers or

---

[1] 1 John 3:2.

authorities; all things were created through him and for him. And he is before all things, and in him all things hold together. And he is the head of the body, the church. He is the beginning, the firstborn from the dead, *that in everything he might be preeminent*. For in him all the fullness of God was pleased to dwell, and through him to reconcile to himself all things, whether on earth or in heaven, making peace by the blood of his cross. And you, who once were alienated and hostile in mind, doing evil deeds, he has now reconciled in his body of flesh by his death, in order to present you holy and blameless and above reproach before him, if indeed you continue in the faith, stable and steadfast, not shifting from the hope of the gospel that you heard, which has been proclaimed in all creation under heaven, and of which I, Paul, became a minister.[2]

Paul recognizes that the fundamental question for every believer is this: what is Jesus' place in your life? Is he, in Paul's Greek, *prōteuō* (πρωτεύω), that is, "to be first, to hold the first rank or highest dignity, have the preeminence, be chief"?[3] The answer has immediate and eternal implications. It determines the direction of our lives on earth and the destiny of our lives for eternity. If the answer is, as it ought to be, that Jesus is first, that Jesus is preeminent, then virtually every aspect of daily life is transformed. Paul's epistle provides a broad yet specific understanding of what it means to make Jesus preeminent.

This book is intended not as a eulogy for my father but as a reflection upon the Jesus who was first in his life at home and at church. It describes what the preeminence of Jesus means in principle, drawing from Colossians 1:15-23, and in practice, drawing upon the example of a father and a pastor. Though my father is, to me, the nearest and most meaningful example of the practice of

---

[2] Colossians 1:15-23.
[3] William D. Mounce. *Mounce Concise Greek-English Dictionary of the New Testament* (2011). https://www.biblegateway.com/passage/?search=colossians+1&version=MOUNCE.

Jesus' preeminence, I am thankful for other authentic believers in the church who have exemplified Christlikeness. Like Paul, these have followed Christ in a manner worthy of imitation.[4] My faith, my understanding of the Bible, and ultimately my relationship with Jesus have been shaped by such obedient, godly examples.

This book recognizes that the next generation needs to see Jesus through the examples of fathers and pastors. In too many Christian homes, fathers give priority to things other than Jesus: to work, to health, to recreation, and to self. Spouses and children suffer the inevitable consequences. In too many churches, pastors give priority to things other than Jesus: numerical growth, financial benchmarks, ministerial recognition, and self-advancement. Families and congregants suffer the inevitable consequences.

A premise of this book is that Christlike leadership in the home and the church are inseparable. This is true for clergy and laity alike. Public character is grounded in private character, and contradictions between the two—spiritual affectation, spiritual hype, spiritual hypocrisy—destroy authority in the home and in the church, breeding cynicism and distrust. Jesus cannot be preeminent in one and not the other, in the home but not the church, or in the church but not the home. The demands of his Lordship are comprehensive and integral. If he is not Lord of all, he is not Lord at all.

That too many fathers and too many pastors relegate Jesus to a role of secondary importance explains, to a great extent, the decline of the Christian family and the Christian church in our country. What happens within the four walls of many Christian homes is opaque to outsiders though evident in disappointing spiritual results. What happens within many Christian churches is more obvious and arguably more disturbing.

The antithesis of the preeminence of Jesus is the preeminence of self. A contemporary term for this is narcissism, a quality of character and mind in which the individual has an exaggerated sense

---

[4] 1Corinthians 11:1.

of self-importance. The biblical term for this is pride. The result of narcissism—of pride—is failed fathers and failed pastors, divided homes and divided churches.

Compounding the problem is the appeal of dynamic, charismatic leaders who are more interested in themselves than in Jesus. "With this sort of celebrity ministry culture," writes theologian Michael Kruger, "it's no wonder that some churches have attracted narcissistic personalities to the pulpit."[5] Both in the home and in the church, what is often sought and expected of spiritual leaders is something other than Jesus. Charisma is preferred over character, attractiveness over substance, man over Jesus. The result is a spiritual vacuum in which Jesus' place is diminished and man's place is elevated. Whereas John the Baptist rightly insisted that "he [Jesus] must increase, but I must decrease,"[6] the proud father or narcissistic pastor insists that "Jesus must decrease, but I must increase."

The solution to the leadership challenges facing both families and churches is to restore Jesus to his rightful place of prominence and priority. This book is a challenge to me—to all of us—who want to make a difference in the home and in the church. It is a call to make Jesus first, in both principle and practice, in word and deed, in thought and action. Jesus defines the wise man—the wise father, the wise pastor—as the one "who hears these words of mine and does them."[7] He defines love in similar terms: "Whoever has my commandments and keeps them, he it is who loves me."[8] Obeying Jesus—putting his principles into practice—is arguably the most loving thing any father can do for his family or any pastor for his church.

---

[5] Michael J. Kruger. *Bully Pulpit: Confronting the Problem of Spiritual Abuse in the Church* (Grand Rapids, Michigan: Zondervan Reflective, 2022), 10.
[6] John 3:30.
[7] Matthew 7:24.
[8] John 14:21.

The next generation is watching and learning from our example, regardless of its character or quality. I watched my father, my pastor very closely and learned from his example. My children and my church are watching me and learning from mine. Your children and your church are watching you and learning from yours. The lessons we teach by example—good or bad—make a difference in time and in eternity. That is why the biblical principles outlined in the pages that follow are so critical to our success—or failure—in the home and in the church. In obedient response to the words of Paul to the church at Colossae, may we strive to live godly and holy lives so "that in everything he might be preeminent."

CHAPTER 1
PREEMINENT IN HIS INCARNATION

He is the image of the invisible God, the firstborn of all creation.
Colossians 1:15

IN PRINCIPLE

Born in 470 AD, Dionysius Exiguus—in English known as *Dennis the Little*, a reference to his humility—was a learned member of a community of monks who resided in present day Romania.[9] Much of his later life was spent in Rome, then the spiritual and cultural center of Christianity, where he combined an interest in theology and mathematics to develop a calendar of key events in the life of Christ, including his birth (Christmas) and his resurrection (Easter). His calculations realigned the calendar around the year of Jesus' birth, though his estimates were imprecise (modern scholarship now places the time of Jesus' birth, based on the date of the death of Herod the Great, between 6 BC and 4 BC). Nonetheless, his contribution was revolutionary. It anchored the calendar—all human history—to the life of Christ, counting the years before Jesus' birth as BC (Before Christ) and the years since Jesus' birth as AD (in Latin, *Anno Domini*, "the year of our Lord"). As a result, the past, the present, and the future are today reckoned in relationship to the incarnation, from historical chronologies to Outlook calendars, from

---

[9] Dionysius Exiguus. https://en.wikipedia.org/wiki/Dionysius_Exiguus.

New Years' countdowns to birthday celebrations. Dionysius Exiguus recognized the fundamental dynamic of time, namely, that all events revolve around the person of Jesus Christ, by whose incarnation God entered and forever changed human history.

Paul anchors Jesus' preeminence in his incarnate reality as "the image of the invisible God, the firstborn of all creation." Jesus embodies the nature, the essence, and the identity of his Father. He shares the image, the likeness of his Father so that, in Jesus' own words, "Whoever has seen me has seen the Father."[10] The invisible attributes of the Father are thus visible in the person of Jesus, the Word which "became flesh and dwelt among us."[11] Without Jesus, we would not be able to see the Father with whom he is co-equal, co-existent, and co-eternal. This is why John, like Paul, bases his defense of Christian faith on his witness of the visible, audible, touchable, historical Jesus.

> That which was from the beginning, which we have heard, which we have seen with our eyes, which we looked upon and have touched with our hands, concerning the word of life—the life was made manifest, and we have seen it, and testify to it and proclaim to you the eternal life, which was with the Father and was made manifest to us—that which we have seen and heard we proclaim also to you, so that you too may have fellowship with us; and indeed our fellowship is with the Father and with his Son, Jesus Christ.[12]

The incarnation is at once majestic and mysterious, a reality confidently embraced by faith yet beyond the full comprehension of the human mind. It is the portal by which salvation is possible, the Son of God entering human experience to save and redeem. It is the path by which Jesus identifies with the frailties of mankind and

---

[10] John 14:9.
[11] John 1:14.
[12] 1 John 1:1-14.

comprehends our sufferings. It is the singular way by which Jesus stands in our place to bear the wrath of God, accepting the death penalty otherwise due our sins. The incarnation—from Jesus' birth to his cross and resurrection—is the axis of history around which everything revolves. The patriarchs and the prophets looked forward with faith-filled anticipation to Jesus' time; those who have lived since look back with faith-filled understanding.

The incarnation represents the miraculous fusion of the divine and the human. It commenced the moment of Jesus' conception, when the egg of his mother was divinely fertilized by the Spirit of God. In that instant, Jesus—fully God—became also fully man, taking an identity he embodied through fetal development, birth, childhood, adolescence, his public ministry, his suffering on the cross, his resurrection, and his ascension. Having "humbled himself by becoming obedient to the point of death, even death on a cross," the incarnate Jesus is now eternally exalted "so that at the name of Jesus every knee should bow, in heaven and on earth and under the earth, and every tongue confess that Jesus Christ is Lord, to the glory of God the Father."[13] In his heavenly glory, Jesus remains forever the Son of God and the Son of Man.

The integration of Jesus' divinity and his humanity was of such importance to the early church that it was the priority theme of the Council of Chalcedon, convened in 451 AD to settle debates about the nature of Christ. Its expression of biblical truth is both eloquent and profound.

> We, then, following the holy fathers, all with one consent teach men to confess one and the same Son, our Lord Jesus Christ, the same perfect in Godhead and also perfect in manhood; truly God and truly man, of a rational soul and body; coessential with the Father according to the Godhead, and consubstantial with us according to the manhood; in all things like unto us, without sin;

---

[13] Philippians 2:8-10.

begotten before all ages of the Father according to the Godhead, and in these latter days, for us and for our salvation, born of the Virgin Mary, the mother of God, according to the manhood; one and the same Christ, Son, Lord, Only-begotten, to be acknowledged in two natures, without confusion, without change, without division, without separation; the distinction of natures being by no means taken away by the union, but rather the property of each nature being preserved, and concurring in one person and one subsistence, not parted or divided into two persons, but one and the same Son, and only begotten, God the Word, the Lord Jesus Christ; as the prophets from the beginning have declared concerning Him, and the Lord Jesus Christ Himself has taught us, and the creed of the holy fathers has handed down to us.[14]

This creed reminds us that the incarnate Jesus was not a phantom who floated over the Galilee for three and half years, above the fray of human existence. He was not a demi-god impervious to human feelings and sufferings. Nor was he a mere man who operated on a human level according to human ability and human wisdom. Jesus assumed his humanity not by subtraction but by addition.[15] He did not relinquish part of his deity to accommodate his humanity, nor did he relinquish part of his humanity to accommodate his deity. At no time in his journey was he anything less than fully God and fully man. Though he humbled himself, even emptying himself of his prerogatives and his rights, he never surrendered his identity, either as God or as man. He took every step of his earthly journey as the Son of God and the Son of Man. He was fully God and fully man throughout his earthly life and ministry, while dying on the cross, and at his ascension.

---

[14] Creed of Chalcedon. https://www.prca.org/about/official-standards/creeds/ecumenical/chalcedon.
[15] mother

PREEMINENT IN HIS INCARNATION

It is precisely at this point that some take pause. "It just seemed too incredible for modern rational and 'scientific' people to believe that Jesus Christ could be truly human and fully, absolutely God at the same time," writes theologian Wayne Grudem. "The kenosis [emptying] theory began to sound more and more like an acceptable way to say that (in some sense) Jesus was God, but a kind of God who had for a time given up some of his Godlike qualities, those that were most difficult for people to accept in the modern world."[16]

Jesus' incarnate identity as "the image of the invisible God" and the eternal "firstborn of all creation" is foundational to rightly understanding Jesus and rightly relating to him. This is the starting point for Paul's passionate argument against the heresies circulating within the church at Colossae. It is the basis of biblical Christology. Get this right, and our theological understandings will be rock solid. Get this wrong, and everything collapses, including spiritual leadership in the home and in the church.

There are two imbalances that can arise regarding Jesus' divinity and humanity, both leading to false conclusions. On the one hand, his divinity can be elevated at the expense of his humanity, making Jesus aloof from human experience and limiting his identification with us. Or his humanity can be elevated at the expense of his divinity, making Jesus more of our equal than our Lord.

In this latter view, Jesus worked his miracles while on earth as a mere man, not as God in his deity; he lived his earthly life with human limitations, laying aside his divinity to fulfill his mission. The punch line follows: if Jesus operated as a man rather than as the incarnate Son of God, he is the prototype of what man, not God, can do. This is another way of saying, "Jesus must decrease, but I must increase." Man is thus on the par with Jesus, and human experiences supplement—or supersede—what he has already done.

---

[16] Wayne Grudem. *Systematic Theology, Second Edition: An Introduction to Biblical Doctrine* (Grand Rapids, Michigan: Zondervan Academic, 2020), 551-52.

Paul's letter to the Colossians was in response to such errors within the church of the first century. While the nature of these errors is not completely defined, they do relate to the ways in which we understand the person and identity of Christ, necessitating Paul's statements on the preeminence of Jesus. One such threat confronting the Colossians was a belief that something more than Jesus was needed to realize spiritual completion, something more than his incarnation, his cross, and his resurrection. This threat persists today in the false belief that something more, something human, something experiential is needed to be spiritually whole: an ecstatic encounter, an emotional high, or a deeper insight. Whether in Paul's day or ours, it is spiritually perilous to place our confidence in anything other than the sufficiency of Christ.

The incarnate Jesus is a wonderful joining of the human and the divine. He is a perfect high priest who sympathizes with us and enters the Holy Place on our behalf. He is a shepherd who can guide us along paths of righteousness for his name's sake. He is a healer who is familiar with our infirmities, a great physician who understands our pain and suffering. He is the second Adam who overcomes the failures of the first. Jesus is at once transcendent in his power and his holiness yet imminent in his tenderness and his nearness. He is both Creator of the universe and humble servant, the beloved of the Father and friend of sinners, the righteousness of God and the atoning sacrifice for sin.

IN PRACTICE

Born in 1935, my father was raised in Decorah, Iowa, a small town about fifteen miles from the Minnesota-Iowa border. A rural, farming community, Decorah is divided by the Upper Iowa River, which cuts through ancient rocks to create a picturesque landscape of steep bluffs and fertile valleys, these in route to its final destination, the Upper Mississippi River.

During the latter half of the nineteenth century, Decorah welcomed a wave of German and Norwegian settlers. Among them was Bernard Dresselhaus (1837-1910), a farmer who emigrated from Westphalia in northwest Germany, his Lutheran faith remembered on his headstone: "Thou, O Christ, art all I want." His daughter-in-law and my father's grandmother, Emma Dresselhaus, was the spiritual matriarch of the Dresselhaus family, coming to Christ during a Salvation Army revival and later joining the local Assemblies of God church. Her strong faith was embraced by her son Elmer, who, with his wife Gladys, would rear three sons—Elton, Richard, and William—on a one hundred twenty-acre farm several miles outside of the town of Decorah.

It is impossible to overstate how much a godly family, a small-town church, and farm life shaped the faith of my father and the preaching of my pastor. His grandmother would spend hours teaching him the truths of God's Word, holding him in her lap as she explained Christ's redemptive plan and foretold his Second Coming. His mild-mannered father modeled a simple faith and prayed simple prayers in keeping with his modest, even temperament. His mother planted the seed of vocational ministry, suggesting to him at an early age that God was perhaps calling him to be a pastor. His family trusted God for their income, which depended upon the sun, the rain, and the soil to nourish the crops. Prayers for divine provision were never routine; the family's livelihood could be destroyed in an instant by a late frost, a hailstorm, or a drought.

Decorah Assembly of God was a small Pentecostal church that was viewed skeptically by the larger, mainline churches in the area. Its status in the community was reflected by its location—on the wrong side of the railroad tracks, literally. Its pastors were biblical but not great orators. The worship was basic and not always in tune; there was no band, no woofers, no spotlights, and no fog machine. The fellowship was intergenerational; those in the youth group, if it existed, could be counted on one or both hands. Given its small size, however, it was hands on, with opportunities for everyone to participate. And participate my father did, putting into practice the disciplines that would serve him in ministry in the years to come.

Home life and church life were intertwined for the Elmer Dresselhaus family. Everyone contributed to the work of the farm, where my dad baled hay, milked cows, and tended chores side-by-side with his father. Everyone participated in family meals and daily devotions. And everyone faithfully attended church. After milking cows—twice daily, seven days a week—and dealing with the sometimes-foul weather, my father's family would unfailingly attend Sunday School, Sunday morning service, Sunday evening service, and midweek service. Often, they would also attend nightly, week-long revivals. Church attendance was not an easy, convenient thing given the demands of farming, the quirkiness of early automobiles, and the unpredictability of Iowa weather. But my grandfather communicated in practice what words could not: Jesus is preeminent, and church is a priority.

There is a reason that Jesus—God with us—spent the great majority of his public ministry in the Galilee. It was not only his home, but it was also rural and agrarian. It provided an open space within which he could walk with his disciples and serve simple people in simple terms, teaching them with illustrations drawn from a world familiar to them, a world created by him. Jesus spoke of vinedressers and vineyards, of sowers and seeds, of shepherds and sheep. He showed that the Son of God was also the Son of Man, one who spoke plainly and was concerned about the little things as well as the big things. The incarnation was displayed by Jesus in everyday situations.

My father's preaching reflected his experiences on the farm. His manner was sincere, authentic, and unaffected. Though articulate and eloquent, his speech was plain and down to earth. In explaining the eternal truths of God's Word, he did so in ways that were understandable and applicable to real life. And, like Jesus, he drew upon daily life on the farm for illustrations.

My father's two pastorates were in urban settings: St. Paul, Minnesota and San Diego, California. For many in these two churches, farm life was foreign. But the lessons from the farm were clear and unforgettable. My father spoke of corn and hay, dairy cows and chickens, tractors and plows, fields and barns, planting and harvesting, good weather and bad weather, plenty and want—all echoing the teachings of Jesus.

Once, when teaching on tithing, he recalled the way in which he learned this timeless principle of stewardship. During his boyhood, his father battled pesty gophers year in and year out. Though nearby Minnesota was celebrated as "the gopher state," local farmers to a person loathed them for the damage to crops resulting from their incessant burrowing. The solution in Decorah and other farming communities was to put out a bounty, paying for each pair of gopher paws. An eager participant in this hunt, my father learned early on that the return on one pair of gopher paws in ten belonged to the Lord. It was a principle of spiritual economy that he would faithfully practice the rest of his life. Everyone in the congregation understood—and did not soon forget—the earthy if not graphic point.

Whether at church to one's congregation or at home to one's family, effective preaching and teaching are strengthened by personal stories that validate in practice what is taught in principle. Jesus' teaching was rich in parables and metaphors that brought home the essential truths he was expressing. As the incarnate Son of God, his mission was both to embody and to communicate truth to mankind, and a master communicator he was. His goal was not to impress but to express in a way that was transformational in the lives of his listeners. His message and his method distinguished him from his contemporaries and astonished his listeners, "for he was teaching them as one who had authority."[17]

---

[17] Matthew 7:28-29.

My father's teaching—both at home and at church—reflected the authenticity of Jesus. His sermons were down to earth because the Jesus he served was down to earth. They were strongly biblical in doctrine and deeply applicable in life. Whether encouraging or corrective, the tone was loving and merciful. He often provided illustrations from his own spiritual journey, candidly sharing his strengths and weaknesses, his successes and failures. He was not above his listeners; he was one of them. The message for others was first a message for himself. If the sermon remained stuck in the ethereal clouds of homiletical abstraction, it was for him a failure. If, however, it struck a chord of conviction and led to positive change, the result was worth the toil.

My father's biblical faith was not complicated. He never pretended to have all the answers, leaving with God things that man can never fully fathom. But what he did know was straightforward. Though well educated (he received his undergraduate training at Luther College in Decorah and graduate training at both Wheaton College (Masters Degree) and Fuller Theological Seminary (Doctor of Ministry)), he was suspicious of the human intellect—including his own—out from under the discipline of Scripture. The parameters of his preaching were the parameters of God's Word; what was biblical was inbounds and what was unbiblical was out of bounds. In this, too, he reflects the incarnate Christ, who was dedicated to hearing and obeying the Father, speaking what the Father told him to say, and fulfilling the purposes for which the Father sent him into the world.[18] If Jesus worked to make sure that he made the Father visible to others, my father worked to make sure that the eternal truths of the Bible were plainly seen by others in both the principles he taught and the practices he lived. As a result, he succeeded in the pulpit and in the home. His Jesus—the amazing Son of God and Son of Man—was on display before his congregants and before his family.

---

[18] John 12:49-50.

My father's view of Jesus—as extraordinary yet down to earth, as exalted yet approachable, as fully God yet fully man—not only influenced his faith but also stimulated his lifelong appreciation of the land of Israel. Over his lifetime, he has visited Israel twenty times, most often leading tours attended by church members and friends. Unlike others, he deemphasized the traditional, often gaudy, pilgrim sites in favor of serene landscapes, unspoiled locations, archeological excavations, and historical vistas that recall the life of Jesus who, as the incarnate Son of God, trekked up and down the same hills, walked the same roads, and crossed the same waters. Jesus' words and actions are not fables or myths but actual history played out on the stage of the first century in a remote corner of the Roman Empire. Just as Jesus left heaven to come down to earth to fulfill his mission, so my father combined reverence for Jesus' heavenly glory with gratitude for his earthly imminence.

While I have many vivid memories of time with my father in Israel—the panoramic view of the Sea of Galilee from atop Mount Arbel, the commotion of bustling crowds on the narrow streets of the Old City of Jerusalem, a moment in time captured in the ruins of King Herod's Caesarea Maritima—one stands out. It is of the two of us sitting on a non-descript wall on the Mount of Olives with the Temple Mount to our backs. It was late afternoon, and before us lay the eastern hills of Judea toward the Jordan Valley. Our time was mostly silent. But it was significant. It was remembrance of an indomitable, lonely Jesus who made one last journey of ascent, sauntering up the dusty and hot Jericho-Jerusalem Road to fulfill his mission on the cross. This was the final, obedient destiny for the Son of God, the Son of Man. He is indeed preeminent in his incarnation—in humility, in grace, in obedience.

CHAPTER 2
PREEMINENT IN HIS CREATION

For by him all things were created, in heaven and on earth, visible or invisible, whether thrones or dominions or rulers or authorities— all things were created through him and for him.
Colossians 1:16-17

IN PRINCIPLE

The worldview of the Bible is based upon the supernatural creation of the universe and of life, especially human life. The first ten words of the Bible explain the origin of the universe: "In the beginning, God created the heavens and the earth."[19] Moses describes the creation of man later in the same chapter of Genesis: "So God created man in his own image, in the image of God he created him; male and female he created them."[20] These two verses define the created order and address our most basic questions about the nature of God and the nature of man. They are foundational to all of Scripture.

This biblical worldview was on John's mind when he penned the prologue to his Gospel, echoing Genesis' first verse: "In the beginning was the Word, and the Word was with God, and the Word was God. He was in the beginning with God. All things were made

---
[19] Genesis 1:1.
[20] Genesis 1:27.

through him, and without him was not any thing made that was made."[21] John tells us that the Creator is in fact the incarnate Son of God. Jesus is the one who spoke the cosmos into existence and breathed life into the first man. Everything exists because of him; nothing exists outside of him.

Paul's understanding is the same as Moses' and John's, that Jesus is the Creator of the universe and the Creator of life. Jesus is the Creator of the cosmos, from miniscule sub-atomic elements to immense galaxies. He is the Creator of all life forms, from the smallest bacterium to the largest whale, from the frailest flower to the strongest tree. And he is the Creator of all spiritual beings, both human and angelic. This establishes Christ's power, a power that comprehends the expanse of the universe, the precision of physical laws, and the elegance of DNA. And it establishes his spiritual and moral authority over nature and over man, who is made in his likeness. Jesus is not disengaged from his creation as deists claim, nor is he on a level with his creation as dualists claim. He is spiritually and morally superior. He is preeminent.

In Paul's mind, Jesus' preeminence in creation is closely and inextricably linked to his preeminence in salvation. He is both "the firstborn of all creation"[22] and, as Paul will soon point out, "the firstborn from the dead."[23] If Jesus is not the Creator of the universe, then he is neither preeminent nor is he Savior. If Jesus is not the author of life, then he is neither preeminent nor is he Savior. If Jesus does not have authority over created beings and over nature itself, how can he possibly exercise authority over sin and death? Paul's answer is resounding: "all things were created through him and for him."

Though the universe "was subjected to futility"[24] because of Adam's sin, Jesus' authority remains unchallenged. Forfeiting the

---

[21] John 1:1-3.
[22] Colossians 1:15.
[23] Colossians 1:18.
[24] Romans 8:20.

option to destroy a rebellious world, God instead sent him to redeem it. This was necessary to reconcile man to God and restore what was lost, anticipating a new heaven and a new earth after Jesus' Second Coming, a return not to deal with sin, as he did in his First Coming, but to consummate his victory and forever establish his rightful dominion, power, and authority. To the Romans, Paul writes, "The creation itself will be set free from its bondage to corruption and obtain the freedom of the glory of the children of God."[25]

The battle of worldviews in our day is, at bottom, a battle over the preeminence of Jesus. It is an ancient struggle triggered by rebellion in the Garden of Eden. It is sustained by clever lies no less satanic than the first uttered by the Serpent to Adam and Eve: "You will be like God."[26] It is contemporaneously expressed in twin lies that drive a wedge between Jesus and his creation: 1) the universe spontaneously happened, and matter came from nothing; 2) man is commonly descended from a single universal ancestor and is not made in the image of God. The twin lies of materialism and evolutionism, under the umbrella of scientific materialism, deny the existence of God. In cosmology, matter explains the origin of the universe. In biology, matter explains the evolution of man. God is irrelevant in either case. Jesus is not preeminent.

On the side of Jesus' preeminence stand the revelation of Scripture, the revelation of nature, and the historic faith of the church. The First Council of Nicaea (325 AD) affirms the biblical worldview and extols Christ as Creator of the universe and Creator of life: "We believe in one God, the Father Almighty, Maker of all things visible and invisible. And in one Lord Jesus Christ, the Son of God ... by whom all things were made, both in heaven and on earth."[27] In opposition to Jesus' preeminence stand "new atheists" like physicist Stephen Hawking and biologist Richard Dawkins, beside them those who signal their position with "Darwin Fish"

---

[25] Romans 8:21.
[26] Genesis 3:5.
[27] The Creed of Nicaea. https://tinyurl.com/259cyx7t.

bumper stickers on their cars, substituting IXTHUS (the first Greek letters of the words *Jesus Christ, God's Son, Savior*) from the early Christian fish symbol with DARWIN. It is all about Jesus' preeminence as Creator, which scientific materialism seeks to erase.

The theological implications of the debate over origins are clear: it is a simple choice between theism and atheism, between God and man. The moral implications of the debate are equally self-evident: it is a stark choice between morality and immorality, between obedience and disobedience, between life and death. Paul makes the connection between the creation and man's moral sensibilities when, against the backdrop of Roman culture's sensuality and hedonism, he writes:

> For the wrath of God is revealed from heaven against all ungodliness and unrighteousness of men, who by their unrighteousness suppress the truth. For what can be known about God is plain to them, because God has shown it to them. For his invisible attributes, namely, his eternal power and divine nature, have been clearly perceived, ever since the creation of the world, in the things that have been made. So they are without excuse.[28]

With the spread of scientific materialism since the nineteenth century, fueled to a great extent by the publication of Charles Darwin's *On the Origin of Species* in 1859, there has been a corresponding spread in unbiblical beliefs and behaviors. Beyond the genocide in the twentieth century at the hands of national socialists and communists, with Darwinian justifications advanced by leaders like Adolf Hitler and Joseph Stalin, there is the ongoing genocide of abortion, the murder of preborn innocents whose lives, though marked by the image of God, are casually destroyed by a culture which has lost sight of its Creator and its identity. This slaughter is the inevitable outcome of the Darwinian worldview. Francis

---

[28] Romans 1:18-20.

Schaeffer cites the example of evolutionary biologist Francis Crick, winner of the Nobel Prize for his co-discovery of the DNA double helix.

> If man is what Francis Crick says he is, then he is only the sum of the impersonal *plus* time *plus* chance; he is nothing more than the energy particle extended and more complex. Our own generation can thus disregard human life. On the one end we kill the embryo through abortion—and on the other end we will introduce euthanasia for the old. The one is already here, and the door is opened for the other.[29]

Other immoral innovations in our day owe their origins to the evolutionary worldview. Alfred Kinsey, the father of the sexual revolution, was an ardent evolutionist and used evolutionary psychology to recast sexuality in terms of animal behavior, biology, and conditioning, fulfilling the promise detected by his high school classmates, who dubbed him a "second Darwin."[30] John Money, who coined the term "gender identity" and brought us the transgender revolution, was also Darwinian and conceptualized gender in fluid, evolving terms. To this august list we must add Karl Marx, who connected historical materialism to Darwinian evolution, concluding of Marxism, "This proposition [is] destined to do for history what Darwin's theory has done for biology."[31]

Given the spiritual and moral stakes of this battle of worldviews, it is perplexing that so many self-identifying Christians would embrace the secular, materialistic narrative of cosmic and biologic origins. Researchers at the Massachusetts Institute of Technology surveyed Americans in 2013 on religious attitudes and beliefs

---

[29] Francis A. Schaeffer. *How Should We Then Live* (Wheaton, Illinois: Crossway, 1976), 234.

[30] John G. West. *Darwin Day in America: How Our Politics and Culture Have Been Dehumanized in the Name of Science* (Wilmington, Delaware: Intercollegiate Studies Institute, 2007), Kindle Loc 105.

[31] Friedrich Engels and Karl Marx. *The Communist Manifesto* (Sonnenahalli, India: True Sign Publishing House, 2021), Introduction.

regarding origins, concluding that a mere 11 percent of respondents belonged to religious traditions that openly reject evolution.[32] This means that almost 90 percent of Americans at the time either belonged to a religious tradition that accepts evolution or did not belong to a religious tradition at all. These data reflect a broad ignorance of both science and Scripture.

How does scientific materialism—both cosmic evolution and biologic evolution—destroy faith in God? It raises the age-old question posed to Adam and Eve, "Did God actually say?"[33] For skeptical Christians who embrace "theistic" evolution, the answer to this open-ended question is that the first chapters of Genesis are simply myth, "an ancient, premodern, prescientific way of addressing questions of ultimate origins and meaning in the form of stories."[34] By discrediting the authority of Genesis, such skepticism ultimately discredits the broad authority of the Bible and ultimately the authority and the preeminence of Jesus. "In my view, there are certain contemporary currents of thought that risk undercutting Christianity as a source of knowledge," concludes theologian J.P. Moreland, "and I shall argue that by its very nature, theistic evolution is the prime culprit. It is one of the church's leading gravediggers."[35]

If the evolutionary worldview contributed to the rise of Stalin and Hitler, of Kinsey and Money, it has surely contributed to the acceptance of progressive cultural norms among evangelicals. Evangelicals who believe in evolution and reject a biblical worldview are more likely to accept homosexuality and less likely to see God as the basis of truth than those who embrace the biblical

---

[32] Eugena Lee et al. "The MIT Survey on Science, Religion and Origins: The Belief Gap." https://tinyurl.com/3ctd8x5z.

[33] Genesis 3:1.

[34] Peter Enns. *Inspiration and Incarnation: Evangelicals and the Problem of the Old Testament* (Grand Rapids, Michigan: Baker, 2015), 29.

[35] J.P. Moreland. "How Theistic Evolution Kicks Christianity Out of the Plausibility Structure and Robs Christians of Confidence that the Bible Is a Source of Knowledge." In *Theistic Evolution: A Scientific, Philosophical, and Theological Critique*, edited by J. P. Moreland et al, (Wheaton, Illinois: Crossway, 2017), 638.

worldview.[36] Further, more than half of evolution-affirming evangelicals believe that abortion should be legal in all or most circumstances.[37] The acceptance of evolution within the church opens the door to the acceptance of the unbiblical values of Kinsey, Money, Marx, and Planned Parenthood.

The casualties in the war of worldviews—the battle over Jesus' preeminence—are too numerous to count. The majority wing of the American church, including the mainline traditions and a growing number of evangelicals, have exchanged Jesus' preeminence for progressive cultural values, replaced the Creator with Darwin, switched the authority of Scripture for the authority of man, and substituted truth with lies. Some have abandoned the faith altogether, their "deconstruction" stories filling the pages of books and spreading across social media and the Internet. These are sober reminders that if Jesus is not preeminent in everything, he will soon be preeminent in nothing.

IN PRACTICE

Though comfortably settled in his first pastorate in St. Paul, in the church where he met and courted my mother, Elnora, and where my younger sister, Ann, and I were born and raised, the tug of the Holy Spirit led him to candidate for the position of senior pastor of San Diego First Assembly in the fall of 1970. The weekend of his candidacy was a whirlwind. On that Saturday afternoon, he conducted a wedding in Wisconsin, drove the long distance back to Minneapolis, boarded a flight to Los Angeles, arrived with his family in the early morning hours of Sunday, then drove two hours to San Diego, only to preach twice for services that commenced mere hours later. On Sunday evening, he was elected. The next day

---

[36] George Barna. "Americans See Many Sources of Truth—And Reject Moral Absolutes." https://tinyurl.com/4v2s5udp.

[37] "Religious Landscape Study: Views About Abortion Among Evangelical Protestants." *Pew Research Center.* https://tinyurl.com/2fsy4r4f.

my parents bought a new home. This all transpired in a little over forty-eight hours. The episode is a window into my father's soul: efficient, diligent, and decisive.

Founded in 1926, First Assembly was a significant, historic church in San Diego. My father would serve as its pastor for thirty-three years, the lion's share of his ministerial career. During that time, he would gain the respect of pastoral peers across the city for his wisdom, his experience, and his leadership. A pastoral statesman, others would turn to him—and he to them—for collegial support.

A fellow minister in San Diego, Tim LaHaye, pastored nearby Scott Memorial Baptist Church. LaHaye gained a national reputation as an evangelical leader and writer, including his authorship of the *Left Behind* series. He encouraged my father during a season of difficulty early in his tenure with these words: "An old preacher once told me that you needed to have the hide of a rhinoceros in the ministry. God bless you as you grow yours."

LaHaye also engaged in the battle of worldviews, the fight over the preeminence of Jesus as Creator. He was instrumental in the founding of the Institute for Creation Research (ICR), serving on its board for many years.[38] In the late 1970s, ICR would host a conference in San Diego, one of whose participants, Ken Ham, would also speak that weekend at First Assembly. At the time an emerging Christian apologist, Ham has since become a lightning rod in the origins debate, sparring in the media with Richard Dawkins and debating Bill Nye the Science Guy. He is viewed derisively by many in the church for his literal and uncompromising approach to Genesis. I do not remember now what he said that Sunday evening many years ago. But I know he contended for the authority of Scripture, for the historical reliability of the Genesis narrative of the creation, and for the preeminence of Jesus as Creator.

---

[38] "Tim LaHaye and the Institute for Creation Research. Institute for Creation Research" (Aug 31, 2016). https://www.icr.org/article/tim-lahaye-institute-for-creation-research/.

This was the message of my father as well, a message clearly communicated in conversations at home and in messages at church. The Bible is true, reliable, and authoritative. It is, from Genesis to Revelation, the comprehensive Word of God. It speaks to contemporary issues with force and clarity, to matters of ethics, morality, and truth. It addresses the origin of the cosmos and the beginning of life. It deals with abortion and sexuality. It is deep yet practical, profound yet simple, timeless yet relevant. My father never held back on matters confronted by Scripture, never shrinking from the hot-button controversies of the day.

Too many fathers and too many pastors unnecessarily defer to "the science" when it comes into conflict with Scripture. Intimidated by language and knowledge outside of their experience, they wrongly assume that the evolutionary claims of scientific materialists are indisputable, in the same category as the law of gravity. This surrender opens the gate to wolves who seek to devour the sheep.

Early on, my father recognized the threat and detected the battle lines of the contest between neo-Darwinian evolutionism and biblical creationism. Before theistic evolution made headway within the evangelical church, he was holding the line. He understood that evolution betrayed the foundational truths of the Bible and historic Christianity, the truths taught by Jesus, affirmed by the Apostles, held through time by the church, and promoted by those who gave rise to the Western scientific tradition. The stark choice is between theistic faith and atheistic doubt, biblical creation and evolutionary dogma, the preeminence of Jesus or the preeminence of Darwin. There is no splitting the baby in the manner of theistic evolutionists, who reject the best of the former and embrace the worst of the latter.

The biblical teaching and biblical example of my father fortified me in biblical truth. Though I would spend my entire adult life in the secular academy—the sanctuary of scientific materialism—as an undergraduate, medical student, physician resident, and medical school faculty, there was never a moment when the essential truths of God's Word were in question. Any resistance I encountered only strengthened my faith, and any conflict over my core beliefs only sharpened my understanding. My experiences in the secular academy and encounters with theistic evolution in the church have forced me to this reasonable and biblical conclusion, a conclusion encouraged by my father and supported by my pastor: "atheistic evolution falls on the sword of extreme—in truth impossible—improbability, while theistic evolution does so on the sword of biblical truth."[39]

Had my father not taught the truth in our home nor preached the truth in the church, there is a possibility that today I would either be a progressive pseudo-Christian or a nonbeliever. If he had not affirmed the reliability of Genesis, I might not today trust the Bible as a source of knowledge and truth. If he had not laid a biblical foundation for my beliefs, values, and behavior, I cannot say with certainty that I would today be a follower of Christ. I can say with certainty that, absent this foundation, I would not be the biblical Christian that I am. If I had not early on imitated my father and my pastor in making Jesus preeminent as Creator, he may not today be preeminent at all.

The sober reality is that evolution has flipped many from Christian faith to atheistic doubt. Their stories are sobering and cautionary. Among them is that of social influencer Rhett McLaughlin, who published the story of his fall from faith on his popular Rhett & Link YouTube channel. In an episode viewed by millions and entitled *Rhett's Spiritual Deconstruction*, McLaughlin describes his journey from full-time ministry to unbelief. The turning point came in 2006 when he read *The Language of God*, physician-scientist Francis Collins' promotion of theistic evolution, which introduced skepticism of the Bible as a reliable source of knowledge. He describes his subsequent journey by analogy to

---

[39] Timothy Dresselhaus. *Seven Deadly Lies in the Culture and the Church* (Springfield, Missouri: ACPT Press, 2023), 62.

pulling a thread in his "sweater of faith," which is reduced first to a vest, then a midriff, then a halter top, then a useless bikini top. "I don't think it is insignificant that the deeper I have dug into Christianity with a thirst for the truth, the more difficult it has become to have faith," McLaughlin concludes. "In fact, for me, it has become impossible."[40]

Such stories are why my father believed biblical truth was worth defending in the living room of his home and in the pulpit of his church. It is also why my pastor believed biblical truth was worth defending in the larger context of his denomination. When he realized—after the fact—that a 2010 update to the Assemblies of God's Doctrine of Creation was accommodating of the evolutionary explanation of origins, he was dismayed. The denomination's *Enrichment Journal* published this disturbing justification: "Pentecostal Christians do not share a single viewpoint on evolution. Pentecostals concur that God exists and is the Creator, but they do not speak with one voice on how ancient creation is, how much evolution has occurred, or whether science provides evidence for an intelligent designer."[41] In two short sentences, the levee of biblical truth was breached. For my father, this was unacceptable and unbiblical. It was not an occasion for compromise or tolerance. This was a violation of the authority of Scripture and the majesty of the Creator. It was a hill to die on. My father worked with others to reverse this egregious doctrinal error. In 2014, the Doctrine of Creation was corrected to include this revised language: "Both Adam and Eve, male and female, are declared to be made in the 'image' and 'likeness' of God ... Any evolutionary theory, including theistic evolution/evolutionary creationism, that claims all forms of life arose from a common ancestry is thereby ruled out."[42]

---

[40] McLaughlin. "Rhett's Spiritual Deconstruction." https://tinyurl.com/fwcc74zr.

[41] Mike Tenneson and Steve Badger. "A Brief Overview of Pentecostal Views on Origins." *Enrichment Journal* (2010). https://tinyurl.com/bdftvs2v.

[42] Doctrine of Creation, Assemblies of God. https://tinyurl.com/4sn33sca.

To remember my father's pastoral career, an endowed fund was established in his honor at Vanguard University, an Assemblies of God institution in Southern California on whose board he once served. When the *Richard L. Dresselhaus Pastoral Ministry Scholarship* was formalized in 2023 to support Vanguard students called to vocational pastoral ministry, it was his wish that recipients hold to the same biblical worldview—a worldview that affirms Jesus' preeminence as Creator—that guided his ministry to his family and to his church. To this end, the scholarship agreement stipulates that "the student must hold and defend, without reservation or qualification, the following foundational biblical truths":

1. God is the eternal Creator of the heavens and the earth—of all matter, time, and space.
2. Man is specially and supernaturally created in the image of God; God did not form Adam from some previously existing creature. Any evolutionary theory, including theistic evolution or evolutionary creationism, that claims all forms of life arose from a common ancestry is thereby ruled out.
3. Truth, revealed in God's Word, is absolute, timeless, and universal.
4. Every preborn life is marked by the likeness of God from conception and deserves the same protection as born life.
5. God designed sexual intimacy to be experienced exclusively in the monogamous, heterosexual, and lifelong union of a man and a woman.
6. God made man in his image as male and female and assigns a sexual and gender identity that is fixed and binary from the moment of conception.
7. Made in God's image, all people share a common essence that eclipses all divisions and all classifications; cultural struggle between oppressed and oppressors based on sex, race, ethnicity, or other group identities should not be

tolerated in the church nor should the pseudo-justice of diversity, equity, and inclusion that accentuates rather than heals conflict and denies the essential likeness of God etched upon each person.

At no time in recent history has the assault on truth been more vigorous. The authority of the Bible is overthrown by the culture and rejected by many in the church. A beachhead in this conflict is Darwinian evolution, which undermines confidence in the Word of God, beginning in Genesis but extending ultimately across the entirety of Scripture. With this in view, I am eternally grateful for my father, my pastor who trusted in his Creator and stood courageously against the majority in the culture and in the church. In doing so, he showed in principle and in practice, at home and at church, that Jesus is indeed preeminent.

CHAPTER 3
PREEMINENT IN HIS CHURCH

And he is the head of the body, the church.
Colossians 1:18a

IN PRINCIPLE

The Edwin Smith Surgical Papyrus is the earliest known study of the nervous system, dating to approximately 1600 BC. In the centuries that followed, a debate raged among anatomists as to whether the seat of human intelligence was in the head (brain) or the chest (heart); others wondered where to locate the soul, speculating that it resided in the liver, adjacent to the gallbladder. It was not until the fifth century BC that the Greek philosopher Alcmaeon fully grasped that the wonders of human thought, bodily control, and sensory perception had more to do with the brain than the heart.[43] This insight is now commonly understood, and the mechanisms of neuroanatomy have been explained in detail, from the mapping of brain function to the molecular pathways across and between neurons.

There is good reason—inspired reason—that Paul used the metaphor of the head-body relationship drawn from human anatomy to describe the spiritual relationship of Jesus to the church. Though

---

[43] Catherine Shaffer. "What is Neuroanatomy." *News Medical Life Sciences* (Jun 14, 2019). https://www.news-medical.net/health/What-is-Neuroanatomy.aspx.

he had no medical background, his broad knowledge and wide reading informed his insight into the meaning of his chosen metaphor. The significance of this anatomical metaphor is highlighted by the continuity in medicine of Greek words used by Paul. His word for *head* is *kephalē* (κεφαλή), from which originate the modern terms *cephalic* (relating to the head), *encephalitis* (inflammation of the brain), or *hydrocephalus* (fluid accumulation in the brain). The word used by Paul for body is *sōma* (σωμα), from which stem the modern terms *somatic cell* (body cell other than germ, or reproductive, cell), *somaticize* (physical symptoms reflecting an underlying mental health disorder), or *chromosome* (the genetic material of living cells). It is possible that Paul discussed medicine and anatomy with his close friend, Luke, whom he identifies as "the beloved physician" at the close of his letter to the Colossians.[44]

What did Paul know about neuroanatomy? He knew that, in relationship to the human body, the head is preeminent. He understood that the head is the center of mind, of intellect, of knowledge, and of authority. By contrast, the body is subject to the control, the impulses, the direction of the head; it is incapable of acting independently or autonomously. Paul knew that any interruption of the communication between the head and the body, as might occur with injuries to the spine or to the extremities, renders the body weak, if not paralyzed.

In Paul's spiritual application, in his statement that Jesus "is the head of the body, the church," he reasserts Jesus' preeminence. Jesus' headship and his preeminence are synonymous. Jesus is first and foremost in his church just as the head is primary in relationship to the human body. What is indisputable regarding human anatomy is indisputable regarding the anatomy of the body of Christ. Both are according to God's design.

---

[44] Colossians 4:14.

Paul's head-body metaphor explains the priority of obedience. Obedience of a human arm or leg to the instructions of the brain is not deliberative but reflexive, not conscious but impulsive. Compliance with Jesus' directions to his church cannot be discretionary or delayed. It cannot be a choice. It must be automatic and immediate. Obedience is the litmus test of authentic relationship to the head. As John explains, "And by this we know that we have come to know him, if we keep his commandments."[45] In John's view, it is impossible to be in relationship with Jesus while disobeying his commandments. This is as certain as the observation that a paralyzed—in a sense disobedient—limb is no longer in proper relationship to the human head.

Paul's head-body metaphor explains the priority of unity. The healthy functioning of the body of Christ requires that all parts operate under the coordinated control of the head. Indeed, this is an operational definition of Christian unity: shared submission to the authority, the headship of Jesus. Christian unity, however, is not unity at any cost. It is not a unity that gives the wink and the nod to sin. It is not a unity that tolerates unbiblical beliefs. It is not a unity that compromises the authority of Scripture. It is a unity that recognizes the preeminence of Jesus in his church. It is unity under his vision, his leadership, and his purpose.

Paul's head-body metaphor explains the utter dependence of the body of Christ upon Jesus. The church can do nothing without the head. If Jesus' Lordship and preeminence as head of his church is in question, the body of Christ is rendered weak or paralyzed. If the church body irrationally claims its independence, futilely endeavoring to act upon its own ideas or exert its own influence, failure is inevitable. This is the folly of man-centered leadership of the church. As to authority and headship, man can never replace Jesus without deadly consequences.

---

[45] 1 John 2:3.

What is true corporately is also true individually. Each individual believer is utterly dependent upon Jesus and subject to his headship. It is not ours to question Jesus, resist Jesus, or disobey Jesus, just as it is not the place of our physical body to question, resist, or disobey the cognitive directions of our brain. The decision to accept Christ as Savior is a decision to accept Christ as preeminent in our lives. It is a surrender to his Lordship as head of his church, his body.

Christian freedom is not the latitude to do whatever we want to do. It is the freedom to operate within the parameters of obedience, within which there is true freedom. It is not the freedom to operate outside the parameters of obedience as defined by Jesus' Word. Later in Colossians, Paul addresses this false, carnal view: "If then you have been raised with Christ, seek the things that are above, where Christ is, seated at the right hand of God … Put to death therefore what is earthly in you: sexual immorality, impurity, passion, evil desire, and covetousness, which is idolatry."[46] The demand of Jesus' headship is that we die to self and to our own desires, impulses, and plans.

Each believers' relationship to the head, to Christ, plays out in the context of the body of Christ, in the setting of Christian community. Just as a finger of the human body is functionally dependent upon proximate structures such as the wrist, arm, elbow, and shoulder, all under the preeminent control of the head, so also each believer functions dependently upon other members of the body of Christ, through which and together with each believer relates to the head, to Christ. It is impossible for a finger to carry out the commands of the human brain if separated from the hand. It is also impossible for a Christian to carry out the instructions of Jesus if separated from his body. A believer who deliberately separates from the body of Christ is disconnected from the head. Such a believer is dying. In view of this, the writer of Hebrews urges, "And let us consider how to stir up one another to love and good works, not neglecting to meet together,

---

[46] Colossians 3:1,5.

as is the habit of some, but encouraging one another, and all the more as you see the Day drawing near."[47]

Outside of the hospital setting, it is not always easy to determine if an unresponsive person is dead. For this reason, cardiopulmonary resuscitation (CPR) is always advised until trained personnel arrive. There is one circumstance, however, when it is plainly futile for bystanders to attempt CPR: decapitation. When the head is separated from the body, the American Heart Association guidelines make the obvious point that resuscitation efforts are futile and unwarranted, relieving bystanders of any obligations to intervene.[48] By logical extension and in keeping with Paul's metaphor, an individual or a church that is separated from the headship of Christ is dead. No other evidence is needed to reach this grim conclusion. Separated from its head, the body of Christ loses connection with its source of life and its sense of direction. It cannot realize its purpose or fulfill its mission. It cannot carry on the work of proclaiming the gospel, healing the sick, encouraging the downcast, or delivering the oppressed. It is aimless and powerless.

Conversely, a church that is strongly connected to the headship of Jesus and submissive to his authority is healthy and strong. Such a church is a formidable force in the world, emboldened in witness and dynamic in power. When Jesus is preeminent in his church, the full authority of the incarnate Son of God and the Creator of the universe is displayed to the world.

IN PRACTICE

The Jesus People Movement transformed the evangelical and Pentecostal landscape in the 1970s. Arising from the tumult of the 1960s, a period of war protests, sexual revolution, and psychedelic

---

[47] Hebrews 10:24-25.

[48] Laurie Morrison et al. "2010 American Heart Association Guidelines for Cardiopulmonary Resuscitation and Emergency Cardiovascular Care." *Circulation* (2010); 122:S665–S675.

drugs, the Jesus People changed the trajectory of Christian theology, evangelism, and music. The epicenter of this movement was Southern California.

It is into this countercultural context that my family would move in 1970. The transition from St. Paul to San Diego was not merely from cold weather to warm weather or from the landlocked Midwest to the coastal expanse of the Pacific Ocean. It was a social and cultural transition as well.

Leaving the one behind was difficult for my father and our family. His relationship to Summit Avenue Assembly of God, his first pastorate, was close and intimate. Summit Avenue was where he met my mother, who, as an organist and pianist at the church, was appreciative of the fact that my father had a car and was willing to give her rides to church in his 1948 Studebaker Champion Convertible; this convenient arrangement quickly blossomed into romance and led eventually to a winter wedding at the church. Summit Avenue was where his two children were born and raised during their most critical and formative years—physically and spiritually. Summit Avenue was home to good friends and spiritual mentors with whom he would enjoy lifelong relationships. Summit Avenue was a warm, supportive congregation who affirmed his calling when he assumed his first lead pastor position at the age of twenty-eight. In short, Summit Avenue was family. In his love and devotion to the body of Christ, it was a difficult thing to uproot from this place of Christian community. It was difficult also for the congregation. One precious woman, Bertha Peterson, who was a grandmother figure in the church and to our family, was so traumatized by his departure—perhaps harboring a sense of betrayal—that she could not say goodbye.

Arriving at the other—San Diego First Assembly—was equally challenging. Though warmly welcomed by a wonderful body of believers, it would take time for relational trust to be established. My father would often observe that it took several years before he really felt like he was pastor of this fellowship. Community is not turnkey.

Like many transplants from the Midwest, my father assumed—in many ways correctly—that California was more culturally and stylistically liberal than staider and more agrarian Minnesota. His first Sunday, he wore his customary suit and tie, as did others in leadership. Then and in the days ahead, this stood in sharp contrast to Jesus People who showed up not in suits or even business causal but in shorts and flip flops.

As a child watching this all unfold, I discerned one thing above and beyond the superficial aspects of dress and style. My father, my pastor loved the church. He was subservient to its head, to Christ, and committed to serving and participating in his body, the church. What he said about the church in the living room of our home and in the pulpit of First Assembly was always edifying. My appreciation of the church derives from his example.

My father's regard for the church was neither naïve nor sentimental. He knew firsthand both the joys and the sorrows of working with people. He experienced the ups and the downs of pastoral ministry. He knew from the inside both the rewards and the costs of serving the body of Christ. But his love and devotion never flagged, perhaps because his eyes were focused not so much on the people around him but on Jesus who is the head of his church. With this view, he regarded serving Christ in the role of pastor a privilege, not a burden.

I have always been perplexed by Christians who have a dim view of the church, an exaggerated awareness of people's hypocrisies or the shortcomings of her leaders. Granted, there are times when people are deeply hurt by others in the body of Christ, by narcissistic leaders or uncaring laity. But this does not negate the essential and vital role of the body of Christ in serving the majestic Jesus who is her head. When I survey my own history, I see many saints who set profound, authentic examples of Christlikeness as I grew up in the church. This perspective was cultivated by my father, who deeply cherished the church in devotion to the one who died for her.

From my father's childhood, family life and church life were merged. They were one and the same. In his small home church in Decorah, Iowa, his family—parents, siblings, grandparents, uncles, aunts, and cousins—were part of the church. But the spiritual bonds with all members of the church superseded these important but lesser bonds of genetic relationship. My father's primary identity was not as a Dresselhaus but as a member of the body of Christ. He regarded as more important his birth into the family of God, accomplished through the regenerative work of Christ, than his birth into the Dresselhaus family. One matters for time; the other matters for eternity.

The same was true of our family's relationship to First Assembly. Church engagement was not *a* priority but *the* priority. Church engagement was the priority not because my father was pastor but because the church was the expression of the Kingdom of God in the world. Church engagement was the priority because it was essential to growth in Christ.

An indicator of how attitudes toward church participation have evolved is evident in a Keith Green song, *To Obey Is Better Than Sacrifice* (1978). A reflection of the Jesus People Movement, Green was edgy, prophetic, and biblical. The inspiration for this song was Samuel's rebuke of Saul for his disobedience in sparing the Amalekite's king and livestock contrary to God's specific instructions (1 Samuel 15:22). The lyrics read:

> To obey is better than sacrifice;
> I don't need your money, I want your life …
> To obey is better than sacrifice;
> I want more than Sunday and Wednesday nights.
> 'Cause if you can't come to Me every day,
> then don't bother coming at all.[49]

---

[49] Keith Green. "To Obey Is Better Than Sacrifice," 1978. https://thescottspot.wordpress.com/2018/02/03/to-obey-is-better-than-sacrifice-1978/

From Green's perspective, church attendance is necessary but not sufficient to be fully obedient to Jesus. But absence from the fellowship of believers—"neglecting to meet together"[50]—indicates not only disengagement from the church but from its head. The refrain "I want more than Sunday and Wednesday nights" is an anachronism to those today who consider it a sacrifice to attend a once-weekly, hour-long service. Such low-level commitment suggests lukewarmness toward God's people and toward Jesus himself.

My father honored Jesus' headship in our home; my pastor honored Jesus' headship in our church. To do one and not the other, in his view, would have been a sham, the worst kind of spiritual hypocrisy. He knew that his credibility at home was the basis of his credibility at church. If he cut ethical corners at home, how could he uphold biblical standards at church? I knew this also: if my father was honest at home, he had credibility as my pastor in the pulpit. If he was dishonest at home, he lost all credibility in the pulpit. In experience, I knew he was completely honest. He would go back to the grocery store if he discovered he had received too much in change; he would reach out to the IRS if there was a tax error in his favor; he would meticulously assure that he tithed on his income and did not steal from God. Watching such behaviors at home, I could honor and receive his preaching at church.

This is in line with Jesus' prerequisites for responsibility in the Kingdom of God and leadership in the church. In his explanation of the parable of the shrewd manager, Jesus elaborates:

> One who is faithful in a very little is also faithful in much, and one who is dishonest in a very little is also dishonest in much. If then you have not been faithful in the unrighteous wealth, who will entrust to you the true riches? And if you have not been

---

[50] Hebrews 10:24-5.

faithful in that which is another's, who will give you that which is your own? No servant can serve two masters, for either he will hate the one and love the other, or he will be devoted to the one and despise the other. You cannot serve God and money.[51]

In Jesus' view, an individual who is dishonest and unfaithful in daily life, including money management, cannot be entrusted with responsibility in the Kingdom of God. Jesus' entrustment of spiritual responsibility to my father derived from his consistent faithfulness in the little things of life, things seen by his family but not by others. The little things are big things in the sight of a child and in the sight of God. They are the building blocks of character and the evidence of integrity.

Deacons—and pastors—are also expected to love and care for their families. "Let deacons be the husband of one wife, managing their children and their own households."[52] It is impossible for a pastor to exercise authentic, godly spiritual leadership who is not first faithful to his wife, not just in a technical, moral sense but in a loving, devoted sense. My father and my mother were one, a unity that stemmed from their oneness as husband and wife before God. My father loved and honored my mother in word and in action, never once undermining her position in our home. He also loved and disciplined his children. He struck a careful balance between affirmation and correction, between encouragement and admonishment. He supported us when obedient and held us responsible when we were not.

Seared in my memory is one particularly defining moment in my relationship with my father. Then seventeen, I was standing in front of our house doing outside work along with my father. A disagreement of some sort ensued, to which I responded disrespectfully. I crossed a line. My father's reasonableness and

---

[51] Luke 16:10-13.
[52] 1 Timothy 3:12.

unwavering patience disappeared in an instant. I saw instead a fierce anger, an affect that rarely registered on his face or in his voice. It was deserved. Had he not stood me down and punished me (my driving privileges were suspended for several weeks), who is to say what downstream consequences may have flowed from a root of arrogance toward my father's spiritual authority? Who knows what downstream consequences may have flowed from a root of arrogance toward God?

My sister and I knew that we were loved but also that we were accountable. Obedience to my father and obedience to God were non-negotiables. Had my father neglected his parental responsibilities, he would have disqualified himself from being our pastor. Had he not been effective in his leadership at home, he could not have been effective in his leadership at church. This inviolable rule of spiritual leadership is as certain as the law of gravity. Its flaunting by too-many fathers of too-many families who are also too-many pastors of too-many churches is at once ethically disappointing and spiritually disastrous.

For my father, pastoral ministry was a calling, not a vocation. While he always made his family priority in his life, his commitment to the local church was 24 / 7 / 365. He did not punch in and punch out. He did not put in the hours and then disconnect. Instead, he loved First Assembly, he ached for First Assembly, he worked for First Assembly, and he cared for First Assembly. He was all in. Why? If Jesus died for the church, then the church was worthy of the full measure of his devotion and commitment. If Jesus loved and cared for the church, so should he. If Jesus gave himself sacrificially for the church, so should he. If Jesus demonstrated mercy and patience toward the church, so should he. If Jesus interceded for the church, so should he. If Jesus taught the church, so should he. If Jesus showed up every Sunday morning, every Sunday night, every Wednesday night, and to every prayer meeting, so should he.

This sense of calling preceded the time when my father derived an income from pastoral ministry. As a graduate student at Wheaton

College, he and my mother attended a small church in the greater Chicago area. He was occupied with studies, and my mother worked to pay the school bills. They were busy. But not too busy to fully involve themselves in the local church. They were not too busy to serve. My father spearheaded the Sunday School program, and my mother helped with the music ministry. Together, they organized teams to clean the church each Saturday in preparation for Sunday services. Had they not been faithful in this way, it is uncertain that they would have been pastors at all, much less the pastors they became at Summit Avenue and First Assembly.

My father understood church governance well enough to know that he was not really in charge. Jesus was. Though he was a capable administrator and effective leader, he never usurped the preeminence that belongs to Jesus. This was displayed in Sunday morning services, where he made ample room for the move of the Spirit and for the participation of others in the life of the church: musicians, lay leaders, students, and children. This often left less time for his messages than anticipated. He never once complained about this, publicly or privately, instead flexibly adapting his messages to the time allowed. I know of no pastor more elastic in his preaching than my father, more facile in compressing a thirty-minute message into fifteen. This flexibility reflected an understanding that the church was Christ's, not his. The platform did not belong to him but to the preeminent Jesus.

My father rejected secular definitions of ministerial success and worldly-wise models of leadership, which seek to make men preeminent. He rejected, in the words of Henri Nouwen, the longing "to be relevant, spectacular, and powerful, the toxic cocktail refused by Jesus in his wilderness temptation but gladly embraced by many pastors today."[53] By contrast, my father regarded himself as a servant, not as the Chief Executive Officer. He sought to shepherd

---

[53] Chuck DeGroat. *When Narcissism Comes to Church: Healing Your Community from Emotional and Spiritual Abuse* (Downers Grove, Illinois: Intervarsity Press, 2020), 25.

people under Jesus, not herd them toward some man-centered, self-serving objective. He did not use his congregants as experimental subjects for novel leadership strategies or faddish marketing schemes. When he needed direction, he turned to Jesus and to his Word, not the Harvard Business Journal. During his graduate work at Fuller, he took a course from C. Peter Wagner, a leader in the Church Growth Movement, who borrowed from the social sciences to create a strategy for success. My father was unimpressed. He was skeptical of anything that detracted from the preeminence of Jesus in the church—or in the home.

For this reason, my father—both in himself and in others, including his children—valued character over accomplishment. He learned this lesson the hard way. While at Wheaton College completing his master's degree in preparation for his ministry calling, his wife working tirelessly to pay his educational expenses, he failed his comprehensives, the final hurdle before graduation. This humiliation meant an anxious and intensive period of studying over the ensuing summer, with everything hanging in the balance. He succeeded in the end, but he learned a painful but critical lesson: tests and trials are the unavoidable avenues by which character and perseverance are achieved, so that "you may be perfect and complete, lacking in nothing."[54]

What success my father experienced was secondary to obeying and honoring Jesus who is preeminent. He knew that if success is preeminent, then Jesus is not. And if Jesus is not preeminent, any success is pointless. Too many fathers in too many homes and too many pastors in too many churches pursue the pointless path of accomplishments over substance, accolades over virtue, appearances over character. Such fathers are more concerned with grades, athleticism, and securing "the American dream" than cultivating spiritual character in their children; such pastors are more concerned with numerical attendance, garnering social media followers, and

---

[54] James 1:4.

hitting financial metrics than cultivating spiritual character in their congregants. By implicitly and explicitly advancing earthly-minded objectives and worldly-wise results, they risk—for their family and their church—spiritual catastrophe. Like the siren song of Greek mythology that lured sailors to shipwreck, the allure of human success—by whatever measure—is an invitation to disaster.

My father assumed the attitude of a servant in the home and in the church. He took to heart the example of Jesus' humility and Paul's imperative to the Philippians: "Do nothing from selfish ambition or conceit, but in humility count others more significant than yourselves. Let each of you look not only to his own interests but also to the interests of others."[55] At home, he was fully engaged in the domestic chores of the household; no task was beneath him. He remains to this day a master in the use of a vacuum. At church, he did not hide in his office or hang out in a green room before or after services. Instead, he vigilantly stood at the main exit each Sunday after service, shaking hands, listening to concerns, hearing of needs—until everyone was gone. After service on Sunday evenings, he tarried to pray with those gathered at the altar. He was never shielded by a security detail and would have declined one if offered. He identified with God's people and preferred them as "more significant" than himself. He was an under-shepherd who always stayed among the sheep. He was protective of others, not of himself. God raised him to be a pastor because he loved God's people. As I survey the landscape of church leadership today, I would suggest this useful and biblical guideline: if you do not love and prefer God's people, you should not pastor God's people.

My father's understanding of the headship of Jesus helped him deal with the criticism that inevitably targets even the most gracious and capable pastor. He cared about people, and he felt hurt when harsh words were aimed at him. But he was never defensive or

---

[55] Philippians 2:3-4.

vindictive, bitter or unforgiving. The measure of his character was not how he handled success but how he handled such adversity.

At other times, he needed to be reminded that Jesus was in charge, that Jesus bore the final responsibility for his church. In the mid-1970s, First Assembly sought to relocate from downtown to a more expansive piece of property central to San Diego. With the support of the board, but under his leadership, the church sold its existing building and bought a bare piece of land without a conditional use permit, without permission to build. Though done prayerfully, it was unnerving for my father. Under the weight of this matter, he sought counsel from a spiritual mentor. Expecting a sympathetic response, he was told instead, "You are afraid of failing." In a moment, he realized that he was the problem—not the project, not others, and not God. His fear stemmed not from faith but from pride. Long after the building project came to successful completion, my father would remember this episode in his preaching. It is a story of weakness and frailty, of fear and doubt. But it is also an example of candor and truthfulness, a reminder that Jesus does not need preeminent men but instead men who make him preeminent. That is my father, my pastor.

CHAPTER 4
PREEMINENT IN HIS RESURRECTION

He is the beginning, the firstborn from the dead, that in everything he might be preeminent.
Colossians 1:18b

IN PRINCIPLE

The Church of the Holy Sepulchre in the Christian Quarter of Jerusalem's Old City commemorates the site of Jesus' death and resurrection. Under the same roof of a church first constructed in the fourth century AD are the sites of Golgotha and Jesus' tomb, according to a very early but not historically certain tradition. The same proximity may be observed at the suggestive Garden Tomb, which stands outside the Old City in the shadow of Skull Hill. What can be said of both locations is that Jesus' cross and Jesus' tomb are close to one another. And just as these two locations are physically proximate, these joined events—Jesus' death and Jesus' resurrection—are closely and inextricably connected. They are, in their adjacency, the twin pillars of Christian hope and the twin apologies of the true, reliable, and historic Christian faith.

Just as Jesus is "the firstborn of all creation,"[56] he is also "the firstborn from the dead." For Paul, there is a straight line between the creation and the resurrection. Jesus spoke the universe into

---
[56] Colossians 1:15.

existence and gave life to all through the creative authority of his Word. He did so out of nothing, *ex nihilo*, "so that what is seen was not made out of things that are visible."[57] Similarly, the crucified Jesus rose again in power and authority, imparting new life to all who trust in him. His power in creation is evident in the beauty and majesty of nature; his power in resurrection is manifest in the beauty and majesty of spiritual rebirth. It is how we become children of God and enter Christ's kingdom.

Paul underscores Jesus' dual authority in creation and in resurrection because they are inseparable. He cannot be the second if he is not the first. This betrays the lethal purpose of Satan's attack on the creation narrative of Genesis. If confidence in the creative authority of Christ is destroyed, so also is trust in his authority in salvation. If Jesus is not preeminent as Creator, he is not preeminent as Savior. If he is not preeminent in all, he is not preeminent at all.

Paul's own conversion came through a personal encounter with the resurrected Jesus. On the road to Damascus to persecute the church, fueled by a murderous hatred of Christians and confident of Christ's mortality, he was blinded by a vision of the living Jesus. Falling to the ground, he asked of the voice who spoke to him, "Who are you, Lord?" The reply forever changed his life: "I *am* Jesus."[58] In this moment, Paul was transformed from one who was dead in trespasses and sin to one who was raised to new life. In this moment, he joined believers of all time in the eternal life made possible by God's love and the sacrifice of the Son: "For God so loved the world that he gave his only Son, that whoever believes in him should not perish but have eternal life."[59] In this moment, he became an apostolic witness of the resurrected Jesus, embarking upon a lifelong and demanding journey that would take the gospel to the corners of the ancient world. Animated by the hope that first confronted him on

---

[57] Hebrews 11:3.
[58] Acts 9:5.
[59] John 3:16.

a dusty road of disobedience, he would later declare, "For to me to live is Christ, and to die is gain."[60]

For Paul, the resurrection is the fulfillment of God's redemptive plan, a plan birthed in the immediate aftermath of the Fall. "For as by a man came death, by a man has come also the resurrection of the dead. For as in Adam all die, so also in Christ shall all be made alive."[61] The incarnate Son of God, the second Adam, entered human history to atone for the sins of the first Adam. The spiritual death that befell Adam and Eve in the pristine Garden of Eden is conquered by the eternal, powerful life that arose from the Garden Tomb.

For Paul, the resurrection is the basis for victorious living. It is practical and relevant to daily life. In his letter to the Colossians, he reminds them that those who have been "raised with Christ" are no longer subject to the earthly, sinful ways in which they once walked.[62] With minds set on things above and lives hidden in Christ, they now "walk in him, rooted and built up in him and established in the faith."[63] To the Romans, Paul expresses his hope that "just as Christ was raised from the dead by the glory of the Father, we too might walk in newness of life."[64] Those who are reborn in Christ not only have the assurance of eternal salvation but victory in the daily battles between right and wrong, obedience and disobedience, Jesus and self.

For Paul, the resurrection is the triumphal hope of the church. For every believer, the resurrected Jesus answers the fundamental and consequential question: "What happens after I die?" Outside of Christ, there is the fearsome inevitability of judgment and death. In Christ, who destroyed "the last enemy," there is the promise of eternal life, of an imperishable body, of the heavenly presence of

---

[60] Philippians 1:21.
[61] 1 Corinthians 15:21-22.
[62] Colossians 3:1.
[63] Colossians 2:6-7.
[64] Romans 6:4.

God.[65] To the Corinthians, Paul underscores the ascendance of the resurrected Jesus, the second Adam, in this parallelism:

> The first man was of the dust of the earth; the second man is of heaven. As was the earthly man, so are those who are of the earth; and as is the heavenly man, so also are those who are of heaven. And just as we have borne the image of the earthly man, so shall we bear the image of the heavenly man.[66]

For Paul, the resurrection is the certainty of our faith. It is the final and transcendent apology. If Christ lives, all counterclaims to his Lordship are put to rest. If Christ lives, all denials of his deity are vacated. If Christ lives, all doubts of his veracity are swept away. If Christ lives, all skepticisms of his supremacy are forever silenced. If Christ lives, everything he has said in his Word, from Genesis to Revelation, is true and binding. If Christ lives, nothing is above him to rival his authority. If Christ lives, he is indeed preeminent in everything. If Christ lives, only one thing truly matters: to "know him and the power of his resurrection."[67]

The all-or-none significance of the resurrection is highlighted in Paul's unblinking examination of the alternative. What if Jesus is not raised from the dead? He writes:

> Now if Christ is proclaimed as raised from the dead, how can some of you say that there is no resurrection of the dead? But if there is no resurrection of the dead, then not even Christ has been raised. And if Christ has not been raised, then our preaching is in vain and your faith is in vain. We are even found to be misrepresenting God, because we testified about God that he raised Christ, whom he did not raise if it is true that the dead are not raised. For if the dead are not raised, not even Christ has been

---

[65] 1 Corinthians 15:26.
[66] 1 Corinthians 15:47-49.
[67] Philippians 3:10.

raised. And if Christ has not been raised, your faith is futile and you are still in your sins. Then those also who have fallen asleep in Christ have perished. If in Christ we have hope in this life only, we are of all people most to be pitied.[68]

For Paul, there is no middle ground on the resurrection. There is no compromise, no halfway, no maybe, no "it's possible, but then again." Either it is a rock-solid historical fact, in which case we owe everything to Jesus, or it is a grand fiction, in which case we are deceived and duped, without hope and to be pitied. If the latter is true, Paul suggests we follow the ancient imperative of the hopeless: "Let us eat and drink, for tomorrow we die."[69]

This is not the conclusion upon which Paul stakes his claim or builds his future. He knows that the historical fact of Jesus resurrection is the linchpin of our faith, the sure foundation of our salvation. Jesus is indeed preeminent in his resurrection and thereby preeminent in everything. Having met the resurrected Jesus and having experienced the power of his resurrection, Paul raises this exuberant declaration, echoing the words of the prophet Isaiah:

Death is swallowed up in victory.
O death, where is your victory?
O death, where is your sting?

"But thanks be to God," Paul concludes, "who gives us the victory through our Lord Jesus Christ."[70]

IN PRACTICE

Several miles northeast of the Elmer Dresselhaus' farm is the Canoe German Methodist Church Cemetery. Surrounded by rolling

---

[68] 1 Corinthians 15:12-19.
[69] 1 Corinthians 15:32.
[70] 1 Corinthians 15:55-57.

hills of corn-bearing farmland, this small cemetery sits beneath the belltower of a white, single-room, wood-framed church built in 1893, near where German Methodists first gathered in an old farmhouse in 1875. Though this church is not associated with the Dresselhaus family, the cemetery is where my forefathers are buried: Bernard (my great-great-grandfather), William (my great-grandfather), and Elmer (my grandfather). It is where my father will one day be laid to rest.

The cemetery is a serene and sobering reminder of the truth poetically expressed by the Psalmist: "For he knows our frame; he remembers that we are dust. As for man, his days are like grass; he flourishes like a flower of the field; for the wind passes over it, and it is gone, and its place knows it no more."[71] We are indeed dust. Our days are like the short-lived flowers of the field. We all die after a very brief sojourn on this earth. Without Christ, this is terrible news. But with the resurrected Jesus in view, the brevity of this life means the imminence of the next.

My father draws inspiration from the examples of the patriarchs Abraham, Isaac, and Jacob. Their passings are remembered with these words: "Abraham breathed his last and died in a good old age, an old man and full of years, and was gathered to his people"[72]; "And Isaac breathed his last, and he died and was gathered to his people, old and full of days"[73]; "When Jacob finished commanding his sons, he drew up his feet into the bed and breathed his last and was gathered to his people."[74] These narratives capture the fullness of life, the closure of death, and the legacy of faith extended to the next generation. My father shares the same realism: his life will someday end, and the baton passed to him will be handed to the next generation. The impact of his life is measured by its continuity between the faith of his father and the faith of his son. His life is a

---

[71] Psalm 103:14-16.
[72] Genesis 25:8.
[73] Genesis 35:29.
[74] Genesis 49:33.

link in a succession of faith that spans the generations from the time of Jesus' first coming to the anticipated time of his second. When he passes, he will join his fathers in the great "cloud of witnesses" who surround the living, cheering them on in the most consequential race of all, the marathon of faith.[75]

I vividly recall standing with my father next to my grandfather's casket in August 1990. At eighty-seven years old, my grandfather had been very active until he died suddenly, likely from an arrhythmia triggered by his known coronary heart disease. As we stood together, we were mindful—and even discussed—that my grandfather no longer had any needs or wants, possessions or belongings, sufferings or sorrows. He did have the only thing that mattered: an eternal relationship with Jesus Christ. In this light, there was a profound sense of victory in my grandfather's completed journey of faith. There was also an awareness that, with his passing, my father's focus was forward to the next generation, to carrying on the spiritual heritage of his father and reliably transmitting this to succeeding generations.

The only reason my father's perspective makes any sense is because of Jesus' resurrection. In this view, there are things that matter more than life itself, and there are things accomplished in time that matter for eternity. The only outcomes of lasting significance—both at home and at church—are lives redeemed by Christ and destined to spend eternity with him. The point of this life is to continue the faithful heritage of past generations into the future. For my father, what matters most is that his children, his grandchildren, and his great grandchildren correctly make the most crucial decision of all, a decision for Christ, securing heaven and avoiding hell. His abiding prayer is that the resurrection power of Jesus would be known and experienced by his posterity. His abiding desire is that Jesus would be preeminent in everything, in both life and in death.

---

[75] Hebrews 12:1.

This desire for his family was expressed at a birthday celebration for his three adult grandchildren—Elise, Noah, and Emma—whose birthdays coincide within a matter of several weeks. "I pray that you will never drift away," he told them. "I pray that when the roll is called up yonder, we'll all be there." He then sang the opening words of a chorus drawn from his childhood at the little church on the wrong side of the tracks in Decorah, Iowa:

Keep me true, Lord Jesus, keep me true.
Keep me true, Lord Jesus, keep me true.
There's a race that I must run,
There's a victory to be won.
Give me power, every hour, to be true.

As a pastor, my father knew that the resurrection is hope not only for the dead but also for the living. Perhaps this is the reason he excelled in officiating funerals and was highly sought by the families of those whom he had pastored, even years after he retired. On the one hand, his messages proclaimed the blessed hope for those who had gone ahead, expressing an eternal confidence in the risen Christ. On the other, he invited his listeners to come to Christ and to put the eternal over the temporal and the heavenly over the earthly. In his mind was the unavoidable calculus of Jesus: "For what does it profit a man to gain the whole world and forfeit his soul."[76] To all in attendance of such memorials, he proclaimed a message at once compassionate and biblical: the preeminence of Jesus in his resurrection as the firstborn of the dead. This message offers authentic comfort to believers whose separation from loved ones is only a brief interlude. "Yes, we are of good courage," writes Paul, "and we would rather be away from the body and at home with the Lord."[77] It also encourages the living who are daily faced with the

---

[76] Mark 8:36.
[77] 2 Corinthians 5:8.

uncertainties and disappointments of this life. In the memorable lyrics of Bill and Gloria Gaither, "Because he lives, I can face tomorrow."

My father's biblical preaching returned repeatedly to the twin themes of the cross and the resurrection. His messages never ranged far from either, to which he was irresistibly drawn time and again. He always kept the cross and the resurrection in view. For him, biblical preaching was built upon these cornerstones of salvation. While Christian growth requires maturity across a broad range of biblical themes, the timeless and eternal foundations of faith remain Jesus' cross and Jesus' empty tomb, quite independent of the longevity of one's faith or the depth of one's experience.

My father's preaching and ministry valued the continuity of Christian history and the legacy of those who have gone before. With the resurrection in view, he grasped the significance of an aphorism shared by a ministerial friend some years ago: "Tradition is the living faith of the dead; traditionalism is the dead faith of the living." His aspiration as a father and pastor was to honor the former and reject the latter. He admired the great preachers of the past—Spurgeon, Wesley, Moody, Graham—and endeavored to learn from them. He valued historical doctrine, appreciating that the faith we today possess has been handed down to us by faithful believers through the ages. He treasured the theological substance of great hymns which lyrically convey the truths of God's Word. And he honored his sacred, pastoral obligation to connect his congregants to the heritage of the past while pointing them ahead to the possibilities of the future, with a vision of the resurrected Jesus before them.

Too many fathers and too many pastors take a short view with a hyper focus on today, as if the elusive and short-lived present is substantive and lasting. They seek to be relevant against the trending measures of success that are uncoupled from both the history and the future of the church. Such measures have more to do with time than eternity, with earth than with heaven. They deny the enduring preeminence of the resurrected Jesus.

During his first pastorate in St. Paul in the 1960s, two teenage brothers whose family attended the church would sometimes sing for Sunday evening service. One was an emerging talent who had his own rock band, inspired by Elvis Presley and the Byrds.[78] His musical ability, good looks, and contagious personality made him a hit with his peers. One Sunday evening before service, sensing that this sixteen-year-old was not on the right track, my father approached him. He gave his life to the Lord that evening. In the ensuing years, Dallas Holm would travel with David Wilkerson, become the front man for *Praise*, release thirty-four gospel albums, win five Dove Awards, and earn induction into the Gospel Music Hall of Fame.[79] What matters most to Dallas, however, is not the accolades but the resurrected Jesus he humbly serves and to whom he committed his life in 1965. This priority is expressed in his best-known single, "Rise Again," the verse of which contemporizes Jesus' promise to his followers: "'Cause I'll rise, again. Ain't no power on earth can tie Me down. Yes, I'll rise, again. Death can't keep Me in the ground."

Not long after that December afternoon in 2015 when my father asked me to speak for his memorial, he also expressed his wish that Dallas sing "I'd Rather Have Jesus," a hymn covered in his album *Completely Taken In*:

I'd rather have Jesus than men's applause.
I'd rather be faithful to His dear cause.
I'd rather have Jesus than worldwide fame.
I'd rather be true to His holy name.

Than to be the king of a vast domain,
Or be held in sin's dread sway.
I'd rather have Jesus than anything,

---

[78] Scott Bachmann. "Dallas Holm & Praise ... Live (1977)," (Feb, 2014). https://greatest70salbums.blogspot.com/2014/02/97-dallas-holm-praiselive-by-dallas.html.

[79] Dallas Holm. https://en.wikipedia.org/wiki/Dallas_Holm.

This world affords today.[80]

My father, my pastor has preferred faithful service to Christ to what this world may afford. He has chosen the preeminent Jesus, the resurrection and the life, the hope for time and for eternity.

---

[80] Rhea F. Miller. "I'd Rather Have Jesus," 1922.
https://hymnary.org/text/id_rather_have_jesus_than_silver_or_gold.

CHAPTER 5
PREEMINENT IN HIS CROSS

For in him all the fullness of God was pleased to dwell, and through him to reconcile to himself all things, whether on earth or in heaven, making peace by the blood of his cross.
Colossians 1:19-20

IN PRINCIPLE

Some centuries after Dionysius Exiguus traveled to Rome to reform our calendar, another monk traveled to Rome on a search whose outcome would be even more consequential. What this young priest saw in Rome during his visit in 1510 disillusioned him, only intensifying his skepticism of the religious practices around him. Not least of these was the selling of indulgences, a practice that falsely promised relief from sins' punishments while conveniently raising revenue for the Catholic Church. Of this journey, Martin Luther would write in disappointment that he had "gone with onions and returned with garlic."[81]

The larger question that preoccupied Luther was this: how is a man justified before God? His practical concern for his eternal destiny was triggered several years earlier when, while riding home on horseback during a thunderstorm, a lightning bolt struck the

---

[81] "The Trial of Martin Luther: An Account." https://www.famous-trials.com/luther/286-home#:~:text=A%20trip%20to%20Rome%20in,for%20resolution%20by%20the%20pope.

ground near him. His cry of "Help!" arose from a soul uncertain of his standing before God.

After this experience—and after his time in Rome—Luther would turn to the writings of Paul for answers to the doubts and fears that plagued him. From his study of Paul's epistle to the Romans, Luther would rediscover the biblical truth of justification by faith in the Christ who died on the cross as the atoning sacrifice for man's sins. Luther would cease to rely on his own works—"filthy rags"[82] in the words of Isaiah—in favor of a righteousness from above, the righteousness of the incarnate Son of God who gave himself so man would "not perish but have eternal life."[83] These insights would inspire the ninety-five theses of protest to the practice of indulgences that he would later nail to the door of All Saints' Church in Wittenburg in 1517, setting in motion the Reformation that has since spread across the world, transforming believers' understanding of the redemptive work of Christ at Calvary.

For Paul, the cross is the central theme of the gospel and the only hope for sinners such as himself. "But far be it from me to boast except in the cross of our Lord Jesus Christ."[84] Paul sees the cross as the signpost of redemptive hope for lost mankind, the solution to the problems of sin and death. It is an invitation extended by a loving, merciful, and gracious Father to a prodigal people who are soiled, impoverished, and dying. It addresses the situation comprehended by David after his adultery with Bathsheba, namely, that he was not a good man who did a bad thing but a sinner—originally sinful, conceived in sin ("in sin did my mother conceive me"[85])—who did sinful things according to his sinful nature. In view of this intractable spiritual dilemma, the cross is good news to sinners—men like David and Luther, people like you and me—who find at its foot a place of forgiveness and eternal life. This is the irresistible attraction

---

[82] Isaiah 64:6.
[83] John 3:16.
[84] Galatians 6:14.
[85] Psalm 51:5.

of the cross, which Jesus would foretell prior to his death: "And I, when I am lifted up from the earth, will draw all people to myself."[86]

Of the Christ who went to the cross, Paul reminds us that "in him all the fullness of God was pleased to dwell."[87] The preeminent Jesus who went to Golgotha was fully God and fully man. Some, offended at the notion of God's death, suggest that the Jesus on the cross was a mere man from whom the presence of God had departed. This is not what Paul teaches. Instead, the incarnate Son of God, the Son of Man went to the cross on our behalf. His essential, incarnate nature preceded, was maintained upon, and continued after the cross. This is the awe-filled conclusion of the centurion who witnessed Jesus' death: "Truly this was the Son of God!"[88] It is the observation of Peter, who, weeks after Jesus' death, would attest to the crowds gathered on the Temple Mount: "… and you killed the Author of life, whom God raised from the dead. To this we are witnesses."[89]

The death of the Son—both of God and of Man—is declared in John 3:16 ("For God so loved the world, that he gave his only Son"), in Isaiah's prophetic vision of the suffering servant ("Yet it was the will of the LORD to crush him"[90]), and in Paul's view of Jesus' death ("He [God the Father] did not spare his own Son but gave him up for us all"[91]). It is also captured in the story of Abraham's sacrifice of Isaac, a narrative graphically depicted by Rembrandt in his *The Sacrifice of Isaac* (1635). In this painting, the great patriarch Abraham, having obediently taken his only son to the top of Mount Moriah to offer him as a sacrifice, now stands above his son, smothering Isaac's face with his strong left hand and thereby extending Isaac's head to fully expose his neck. He is coiled to bring down upon Isaac the blade which he holds in his right hand, held high above his head. Fully prepared to do the terrible deed

---

[86] John 12:32.
[87] Colossians 1:19.
[88] Matthew 27:54.
[89] Acts 3:15.
[90] Isaiah 53:10.
[91] Romans 8:32.

(reasoning, according to Hebrews, "that God was able even to raise him from the dead"[92]), the slitting of Isaac's throat is prevented by an angelic hand which grabs Abraham's right wrist to arrest its forward progress. The prophetic forecast of this passage is suggested in the ensuing verses:

> And Abraham lifted up his eyes and looked, and behold, behind him was a ram, caught in a thicket by its horns. And Abraham went and took the ram and offered it up as a burnt offering instead of his son. So Abraham called the name of that place, 'The LORD will provide"; as it is said to this day, "On the mount of the LORD it shall be provided.[93]

What did God provide on the top of Mount Moriah? A substitute. A ram, yes, but in truth his own Son. What God prevented Abraham from doing to his son he would do to his own. He would spare Abraham's son but not spare his Son. This reality is incomprehensible to any father and offensive to the modern mind. But it is the only and extravagant way that the eternal love of God, expressed in the sacrifice of his only Son, could rescue man from the death that inevitably follows sin. This is the reality of the cross.

The cross is how God, through Christ, worked to "reconcile to himself all things."[94] Whereas the sin of the first Adam brought death and suffering not only to the first couple but to the creation, the atoning death of the second Adam brings life and hope. Whereas the sin of the first Adam separated man from God, the atoning death of the second Adam restores man's broken relationship with God.[95] This process of reconciliation is started by God; it is of his initiative, not ours. This process of reconciliation is completed by God; it is accomplished by Jesus, not by any human effort.

---

[92] Hebrews 11:19.
[93] Genesis 22:13-14.
[94] Colossians 1:20.
[95] Romans 5:12-21; 1 Corinthians 15:20-23, 42-49.

Charles Spurgeon (1834-1892), remembered as "The Prince of Preachers" for his convicting biblical messages, frequently visited the cross in his preaching to his London congregation at New Park Street Chapel. He boldly upheld the teachings of Paul and the Reformed tradition of Luther in his emphasis on Jesus' substitutionary atonement.

> Jesus has borne the death penalty on our behalf. Behold the wonder! There He hangs upon the cross! This is the greatest sight you will ever see. Son of God and Son of Man, there He hangs, bearing pains unutterable, the just for the unjust, to bring us to God. Oh, the glory of that sight! The innocent punished! The Holy One condemned! The Ever-blessed made a curse! The infinitely glorious put to a shameful death. The more I look at the sufferings of the Son of God, the more sure I am that they must meet my case. Why did He suffer, if not to turn aside the penalty from us? If, then, He turned it aside by His death, it is turned aside, and those who believe in Him need not fear it.[96]

Paul reminds the Colossians that, aside from the blood of Jesus, there is no cleansing from the stain of sin, no answer to the fear of death, no resolution of man's separation from God. Without the shed blood of Jesus, there would be no hope for Saul on the Damascus Road or for Luther returning from Rome. Without the shed blood of Jesus, there is no hope for us. But because of the blood of Jesus, flowing freely from the One in whom "all the fullness of God was pleased to dwell," God has made "peace by the blood of his cross." This is why the answer to the hymnist's question—"What can wash away my sin?"—is singular and absolute: "Nothing but the blood of Jesus." There is no other way to the Father. There is no other

---

[96] Charles H. Spurgeon. "Spurgeon Quotes." https://www.princeofpreachers.org/quotes/category/the-cross.

forgiveness of sin. There is no other eternal life but through the cross of the preeminent Jesus.

IN PRACTICE

In 1857, the Norwegian Evangelical Lutheran Church established a seminary to supply ministers for Norwegian congregations in the Midwest comprised of newly arrived immigrants. Initially located in St. Louis, the school would relocate first to La Crosse, Wisconsin before its final move in 1861 to Decorah, Iowa. Situated in a scenic valley alongside the Upper Iowa River, Luther College would carry on the Reformed tradition of its namesake.[97]

Though my father's spiritual roots are traceable to the Azusa Street Revival that launched the Pentecostal movement of the twentieth century and gave rise to Decorah Assembly of God, his decision to attend hometown Luther College would also shape his theology. From Luther's theology and Luther's grasp of the epistle to the Romans, he would gain a fuller appreciation of the significance of the cross and would understand that man is justified by faith and not by works. The cross was central to my father's leadership in the home and preaching in the church. In personal devotions and public messages, he always stayed close to the cross, regardless of the Bible passage that he was then expositing. On many occasions, he would repeat Paul's words, as translated in the King James Version familiar from his youth: "But God forbid that I should glory, save in the cross of our Lord Jesus Christ."[98]

The cross was visibly prominent in the sanctuary of First Assembly, which was constructed in 1976 during the early days of his ministry in San Diego. A cross stood atop a grand arch that spanned the entrance to the church's foyer. A cross was also the visual focus of the sanctuary, prominent on the back wall of the platform. And a wooden cross was centered on the front of the

---

[97] "Luther College (Iowa)." https://en.wikipedia.org/wiki/Luther_College_(Iowa).
[98] Galatians 6:14, KJV.

pulpit, raised before God's people as the Word was declared each week. What was physically true of these crosses at First Assembly was spiritually true of my father's ministry. This iconography, incorporating crosses into the structure and décor of the church itself, was a visible reminder of the priority of the cross, of the preeminence of Jesus in his suffering on our behalf. My father understood that the only solution to everyone's sin problem was the cross, that the only answer to the fear of death was the cross, and that the only means of eternal life was the cross. His focus on the preeminent Jesus, who once bled upon a cross on his behalf, is lyrically expressed by Fanny Crosby:

Jesus, keep me near the cross;
There a precious fountain,
Free to all, a healing stream,
Flows from Calvary's mountain.

In the cross, in the cross,
Be my glory ever,
Till my raptured soul shall find
Rest beyond the river.[99]

My father lamented the absence of the cross from the contemporary church, both physically and spiritually. Too many pastors of too many churches have removed the cross from the sanctuary, replacing it with projection screens or black backdrops to enhance the effect of sophisticated lighting. More significantly, they have removed the cross from their preaching. Perhaps it arises occasionally—especially around the time of Easter. But it is not preeminent. It is not first. Preaching is sanitized of references to the sufferings of Christ, the blood of Christ, the agony of Christ. This

---

[99] Fanny Crosby. "Near the Cross." https://en.wikipedia.org/wiki/Near_the_Cross.

shift depreciates the sacrifice of God's Son and underestimates the true depth of the problem of sin.

My father embraced the priority of Paul, of Luther, and of Spurgeon upon the cross. He fully agreed with Spurgeon, whose emphasis on the cross stands in sharp contrast with the often cross-less preaching of our day:

> On whatever subjects I may be called to preach, I feel it to be a duty which I dare not neglect to be continually going back to the doctrine of the cross—the fundamental truth of justification by faith which is in Christ Jesus. This topic is essential to the life of the soul. [100]

My father appreciated, with Spurgeon, that the blood shed by Jesus on the cross was the only hope, the only remission of sins. Any preaching that moved away from the cross was worthless, even idolatrous. If the crucified Christ is not lifted up to draw men to himself, then who or what is?[101] If anyone other than Jesus is lifted up, placing Jesus in a subsidiary position, it is idolatry. If any message other than Jesus is lifted up, placing the gospel in a subordinate position, it is idolatry. This was the temptation to the church at Colossae, to the Catholic Church of Luther's day; it is the temptation to the church in our day. Will we give Jesus his rightful place of preeminence, including his elevated and exalted position as the Christ who suffered on the cross, or will we advance a false, idolatrous substitute? When the church does the latter, it is divorced from the kingdom, the power, and the glory of Jesus.

My father, my pastor frequently invited his family and his congregants to come to the altar, to come to the cross. Altar calls were the rule rather than the exception in his ministry. These were opportunities to experience forgiveness, healing, and restoration

---

[100] Charles H. Spurgeon. "Spurgeon Quotes." https://www.princeofpreachers.org/quotes/category/the-cross.

[101] John 12:32.

from the Savior, to kneel at the foot of the cross. It was there that burdens fell aside, sins were washed away, and hearts were mended. Such moments—whether at Summit Avenue, or at First Assembly—are indelibly etched in my memory, coupled with images of my father praying over his family and my pastor praying over his congregation. They were crucial in their significance and far-reaching in their consequences, for they invited the power of the cross into my life and into the lives of others in my family and in my church.

My father gave priority to the celebration of communion, which was a regular and significant part of Sunday morning services throughout his tenures as pastor. He took seriously Jesus' imperative, "Do this in remembrance of me."[102] Of all the things that Jesus could have instituted for the purpose of remembrance, he chose the eating of the bread and the drinking of the cup that at once fulfilled the Passover inaugurated at Mount Sinai more than a millennium before and anticipated his imminent death on the cross. The bread and the wine are succeeded by his body and his blood, establishing "the new covenant in my [Jesus'] blood."[103] In this way Jesus signals the primacy of the cross in the life of every believer, as the basis of a new covenant with man that depends solely on Christ's work on our behalf.

My father also understood that the implications of the cross extend beyond the initial experience of conversion. Paul knew this also: "But far be it from me to boast except in the cross of our Lord Jesus Christ, *by which the world has been crucified to me, and I to the world.*"[104] The call to follow Christ is a call also to die with Christ, to take up our cross and follow him. It is a call to deny self and to live for him. The "cross life," as my father would often term it, is a daily determination to die and a recognition of total dependency upon the ongoing work of Christ. The cross embraces

---

[102] Luke 22:19.
[103] Luke 22:20.
[104] Galatians 6:14.

both justification and sanctification, encompassing both the first step of repentance of sin and the ongoing commitment to crucify the sinful nature which still lurks within.

The continuity of justification and sanctification are emphasized in Paul's epistle to the Romans and fundamental to Luther's theology, as it was to my father's. As one contemporary commentator has observed, with an eye toward Luther's understanding of Romans:

> Justification turns on how the believer appears in the sight of God when he or she comes to faith, while sanctification starts with one's awareness of the vast chasm between this lack of holiness and the holiness of God. Sanctification is then one's attempt in cooperation with God to achieve movement from one's current waywardness and rebellion toward the holiness of God."[105]

My father's preaching advanced this balanced perspective on the twin doctrines of justification and sanctification. He also sought balance in his related teaching on faith and works. While works contribute nothing to justification, they are invariably produced in the context of sanctification and in cooperation with the ongoing work of the Holy Spirit. My father's ministry at home and at church echoed this practical Protestant aphorism: "Faith alone is what justifies, but the faith that justifies is not alone."[106]

Illustrative of my father's laser focus on Jesus' cross is the extraordinary effort put forth to assure that a favorite hymn, "And Can It Be," was incorporated into the existing hymnals at San Diego First Assembly in the early 1970s. My father was disappointed that this marvelous hymn was not among those in this book. The solution? Make copies of "And Can It Be" and glue them into every one of the hundreds of hymnals. This tedious task was completed

---

[105] Glen W. Menzies. *Romans, Pentecostal New Testament Commentaries* (Eugene, Oregon: Wipf & Stock, forthcoming), 11.
[106] Menzies, *Romans*, 12.

through pain-staking printing, cutting, and pasting. But soon thereafter, an observant staff member pointed out that "And Can It Be" was in fact already in the hymnal—on page 201! Through this oversight and tremendous exertion, the words of this hymn were twice stated in the same hymnal. But perhaps this is itself a worthy outcome and indicative of my father's commitment to the priority of the cross and the preeminence of Jesus, poetically expressed in the incomparable lyrics of Charles Wesley (1738):

> And can it be that I should gain
> An int'rest in the Savior's blood?
> Died He for me, who caused His pain?
> For me, who Him to death pursued?
> Amazing love! How can it be
> That Thou, my God, shouldst die for me?
> Amazing love! How can it be
> That Thou, my God, shouldst die for me?

CHAPTER 6
PREEMINENT IN HIS MERCY

And you, who once were alienated and hostile in mind, doing evil deeds, he has now reconciled in his body of flesh by his death, in order to present you holy and blameless and above reproach before him.
Colossians 1:21-22

IN PRINCIPLE

Man's true spiritual situation is characterized in the first chapters of Genesis, which establishes both man's unconditional value as created in the image of God (*Imago Dei*) and, after the Fall, his great spiritual need as originally sinful (*peccatum originale*). The language of "original sin" was not specifically defined until the time of Augustine of Hippo (354-430 AD), who was first to use the phrase. The Councils of Carthage (411-418 AD) incorporated Augustine's biblical viewpoint to counteract the false teachings of Pelagius, expressed in 411 by his friend Caelestius, who asserted that "even if Adam had not sinned, he would have died," that "Adam's sin harmed only himself, not the human race," and that "the whole human race neither dies through Adam's sin or death, nor rises again through the resurrection of Christ."[107] Caelestius—and

---

[107] Daniel J. Castellano. "The Origins of Original Sin." https://www.arcaneknowledge.org/catholic/original3.htm.

those who embraced Pelagianism—violated the clear teachings of Moses, Jesus, and Paul. The entire redemptive plan, launched in response to Adam's sin and completed by Jesus at the cross, rests upon the original, deadly, and pervasive impact of Adam's sin.

Sin effaces the image of God and shatters man's relationship to God. The original sin of Adam and Eve forever altered physical and spiritual reality. Shame replaced innocence, fear supplanted peace, death displaced life, disobedience overtook obedience, and separation from God superseded fellowship with God. Ejected from the Garden, the relationship of the first couple to God was entirely broken, both in their physical and in their spiritual separation from him. This estrangement has been man's natural—original—state ever since.

Paul puts the blame squarely on Adam and his descendants, whom he declares in his letter to the Colossians are "alienated and hostile in mind, doing evil deeds." This relational enmity is compared elsewhere in Scripture to harlotry, political insurrection, and even regicide. Unlike other broken relationships in human experience, the responsibility in this case falls solely upon man, not God. Incredibly, the impetus for restoration arises not from the offender but the offended.

Against this backdrop of conflict, Paul twice speaks of "reconciliation" as he comprehends the full meaning of the cross and the doctrine of atonement. That we are reconciled to God through Christ presupposes a broken relationship. Man's essential condition, in Paul's view, is one of rebellion against the Lordship of Christ and surrender to his adversary. To his opponents, to all who are anti-Christ, Jesus himself unequivocally declares, "You are of your father the devil, and your will is to do your father's desires."[108]

What would possibly motivate God to seek reconciliation in the face of such hostility? It is certainly *not* that man is so lovely and wonderful. Nor is man doing God a special favor by reopening the

---

[108] John 8:44.

lines of communication as if God has some unmet need that only man can fill. God's motivation can only be grasped—and incompletely so—by recognizing the extravagance of his love and mercy. The depth of his love is unfathomable, the extent of his mercy unmeasurable. "The steadfast love of the LORD never ceases," writes Jeremiah, "his mercies never come to an end; they are new every morning; great is your faithfulness."[109]

Jesus' preeminence in the cross reflects his preeminence in love and in mercy. The two go hand in hand. God's love divorced from his justice would be permissive; God's justice divorced from his love would be crushing. The cross is a signpost of both. Of God's love for sinful man, John famously writes: "For God so loved the world that he gave his only Son."[110] Of the just penalty that Jesus would eventually bear, Isaiah writes: "Yet it was the will of the LORD to crush him."[111] Jeremiah also anticipates Jesus' sufferings when he speaks of "the cup of the wine of [God's] wrath,"[112] a cup of which Jesus asked, "My Father, if it be possible, let this cup pass from me; nevertheless, not as I will, but as you will."[113]

Jesus drank that cup of God's wrath to satisfy God's justice. Jesus was persecuted by the Romans, but he was prosecuted by God. Many have suffered and died on a cross, including the two thieves crucified alongside Jesus. But no one has experienced the divine justice that fell upon Jesus, the weight of which began to press him at Gethsemane, where he sweat blood.[114] The justice of Calvary is eloquently expressed by the great British preacher, Martyn Lloyd-Jones:

> Look again at the cross, my friend. Take another survey. Examine it again with greater depth and profundity and having seen the

[109] Lamentations 3:22-23.
[110] John 3:16.
[111] Isaiah 53:10.
[112] Jeremiah 25:15.
[113] Matthew 26:39.
[114] Luke 22:44.

grace and the mercy and the compassion and the kindness of God, look again and this is what you will see. You will see the righteousness of God. You will see the justice of God and his holiness. It is the place of all places in the universe where these attributes of God can be seen most plainly.[115]

Mercy is God's extension, in the crucified Son of God, of divine relief from the wages of sin, which are death. Except for this mercy, it would be ours to drink the cup of wrath and die upon a cross. Jesus' death foreshadows the fate that would befall us were it not for his loving gift of mercy. Were it not for his mercy, Jesus would not have been crushed. Were it not for his mercy, we would be crushed. The relief from the death penalty otherwise incurred is captured later in Paul's epistle to the Colossians, when he writes:

> And you, who were dead in your trespasses and the uncircumcision of your flesh, God made alive together with him, having forgiven us all our trespasses, by canceling the record of debt that stood against us with its legal demands. This he set aside, nailing it to the cross.[116]

If love and mercy are the divine motives behind the cross, what is their intended result? Paul states it succinctly: "… in order to present you holy and blameless and above reproach before him." This is the effect, the outcome of what Christ accomplished on the cross. Jesus' blood not only washes away every sin but also covers us with his righteousness. How else can we approach the presence of the holy God in his throne room? The writer of Hebrews explains our access this way:

---

[115] Martyn Lloyd-Jones. "Why the Cross?" *CultureWatch* (Apr 15, 2017). https://billmuehlenberg.com/2017/04/15/why-the-cross/.
[116] Colossians 2:13-14.

Therefore, brothers, since we have confidence to enter the holy places by the blood of Jesus, by the new and living way that he opened for us through the curtain, that is, through his flesh, and since we have a great priest over the house of God, let us draw near with a true heart in full assurance of faith, with our hearts sprinkled clean from an evil conscience and our bodies washed with pure water.[117]

Someday soon, whether by death or by Jesus' imminent return, each of us—great and small—will pass from this life and will be ushered into the courtroom of heaven. God himself will be seated on a throne from which he will render a final verdict to each person in attendance: "And just as it is appointed for man to die once, and after that comes judgment."[118] On hand will be books that record everything ever done by every person present. All will be held to account for everything written in these books, with one eternally significant exception: those names entered in another book, *The Book of Life*. Each entry in this latter book is written in Jesus' blood, was paid for by his blood. This blood is the only way to the eternal presence of God in heaven and the only exception to eternal separation from God in hell.[119]

Jesus is preeminent in his merciful cross, a cursed tree upon which he purchased our salvation, so that he might be preeminent in everything.

IN PRACTICE

A memorable moment during my father's tenure at San Diego First Assembly was the visit of Corrie ten Boom, not long before her death in 1983. A Dutch watchmaker, Corrie and her Christian family would risk their lives to hide Jews from the Nazis who had invaded

---

[117] Hebrews 10:19-22.
[118] Hebrews 9:27.
[119] Revelation 20:11-15; 2 Corinthians 5:10; Romans 14:10.

her homeland. This brave defiance of Hitler's regime—recounted in the book-turned-movie *The Hiding Place*—would end in her family's arrest by the Gestapo in February 1944. Though those hidden in her home were saved, her family was not: her father would die in prison shortly thereafter as eventually would her sister. In December 1944, Corrie was released from the Ravensbrück concentration camp due to an administrative error.[120] Days later, all the women her age were gassed.

On the Sunday evening of her visit to our church, against this backdrop of immense courage in the face of unspeakable evil, Corrie illustrated the lesson of her life with a sample of her embroidery, holding up the canvas for all to see. She first displayed the underside, revealing a tangled knot of threads. This, she said, is life as we see it: messy, confusing, and chaotic. She then turned over the hoop, revealing a delicate and beautiful pattern. This, she said, is life as God sees it, according to his unfolding plan and purposeful design. She reminded us that God's perspective is not ours and that his ways are not always our ways.

For her, the tangled underside of life was real. She had struggled to reconcile God's love with the cruelty that she had experienced. She wrestled with forgiving the ruthless guards who had stripped her of her dignity and taken her sister's life. She recalls a critical moment not long after her release when she met a former guard after a service in Germany at which she had spoken of forgiveness. She describes her flashback this way: "It came back with a rush: the huge room with its harsh overhead lights, the pathetic pile of dresses and

---

[120] Kaylena Radcliff. "A War Story: 'There Is No Pit So Deep God's Love Is Not Deeper Still.'" *Christian History Magazine* (2017). https://christianhistoryinstitute.org/magazine/article/there-is-no-pit-so-deep.

[121] Corrie ten Boom. "Guideposts Classics: Corrie ten Boom on Forgiveness." *Guideposts* (November, 1972). https://guideposts.org/positive-living/guideposts-classics-corrie-ten-boom forgiveness/.

shoes in the center of the floor, the shame of walking naked past this man."[121] The guard approached her without recognizing her from his time at Ravensbrück. "'A fine message, *fräulein*! How good it is to know that, as you say, all our sins are at the bottom of the sea!' And I, who had spoken so glibly of forgiveness, fumbled in my pocketbook rather than take that hand." Praying silently for Jesus' help amid the swirl of conflicting emotions, she extended her hand to her former tormentor.

> And as I did an incredible thing took place. The current started in my shoulder, raced down my arm, sprang into our joined hands. And then this healing warmth seemed to flood my whole being, bringing tears to my eyes. "I forgive you, brother!" I cried. "With all my heart!" For a long moment we grasped each other's hands, the former guard and the former prisoner. I had never known God's love so intensely as I did then.

This is mercy operationalized: the expression to another of God's forgiveness of us. It is bringing others to the foot of the cross, to a shared experience of God's sacrificial love.

If there is one quality that characterized my father's life at home and his ministry at church, it was mercy. He was widely known as a merciful man, some even suggesting that he had "the gift of mercy." Though he never suffered the indignities of a German concentration camp, he had ample opportunities to display this grace in his relationships to others.

My father's response to offenses and slights was to extend mercy rather than seek retribution. While he understood that there is a role for correction and restitution, he also understood that mercy should always lead the way. This inclination sometimes vexed those close to him, myself included, who wanted to stand in his defense, to settle the score, and to see justice satisfied. But my father knew that if Jesus was preeminent in mercy toward him, mercy must be preeminent in his response to others. Mercy shown flows from mercy received.

Mercy started in his relationships at home, and I was a frequent beneficiary. He did not neglect his duty to discipline and correct, but he always did so through the lens of mercy. Even in the face of failings on my part, whether willful disobedience or honest mistakes, he was unfailingly patient. I recall one instance of the latter, occurring when I was a teenager. My father had just purchased a new car, which was sparkling as it sat safely in the garage. To the side, hung from the ceiling of the garage, was a bicycle. When I decided one day to take a ride, I carefully lifted the bike from the hooks on which it was suspended, only to lose control, dropping the handlebar squarely on the roof of my father's hitherto pristine vehicle. I felt ridiculous and guilty as I stood with my head sticking through the bike's frame. After freeing myself, I reported the unfortunate episode to my father. I knew this was disappointing news. But his response was measured and understanding. I was not demeaned nor was I brow beaten. I grasped the gravity of my mistake but was not made to feel stupid. My father displayed mercy.

On the flip side, my father often sought mercy … from me! My mind retains the indelible impressions of not one, not a few, but many times that he apologized to me when he felt that he had, as a father, fallen short in attitude or in conduct. He was exquisitely sensitive to the conviction of the Holy Spirit in this regard and unfailingly rectified this by apologizing and requesting forgiveness. He did not excuse, justify, or whitewash his failings, however minor. He confessed them and asked forgiveness. Had he not sought and received mercy in this way, he would not have so unfailingly and authentically displayed it in his leadership outside of the home.

In his ministry to others, my father was longsuffering just as he had been when I dropped a bike on his new car. He never responded in kind. Early in his tenure at San Diego First Assembly, he was the subject of a disinformation campaign, launched by critics who sought to discredit him by sending malicious letters to congregants and even to other pastors in the area. Though this was deeply painful to him, he did not publicly defend himself nor harbor ill-will toward those behind this effort. He would, over the years, win them back and recover their trust. He did so through mercy. He did so by extending to others the forgiveness that Jesus extended to him. He did so by appreciating the sacrifice that Christ made on the cross—for him and for others. As his preaching returned time and again to the cross, he stood first in its shadow to experience its love and mercy. This transformed his demeanor toward others, whom he saw through the eyes of God's love and mercy, first expressed to him in order to be expressed to others. In doing so, he participated in the double blessing described by Shakespeare: "It [mercy] blesseth him that gives and him that takes."[122]

Mercy was also expressed in his compassion toward others. This was seen in his identification with the marginalized in his congregation, those without power or influence, those who were misfits in the church. He was always kind to such individuals, making extra effort to notice them, to talk to them, to listen to them. My mind is filled with colorful pictures of such individuals, individuals whom the world otherwise passes by. And my mind is filled with images of my father engaging them, a kind expression on his face, a genuine warmth as he shook their hands. This is mercy. This is the preeminence of Jesus in my father, my pastor.

"When someone claims they know God," observes Alistair Begg, "the veracity of the statement will not be revealed in the breadth of their theological understanding but will be revealed in the depth of their modeled transformation."[123] This was true of my father's example not only of mercy but also of a life that was "holy and blameless and above reproach."[124] He understood the cross well enough to know that he was not justified by his conduct. But he also

---

[122] William Shakespeare. *The Merchant of Venice* (Act 4, Scene 1).
[123] Alistair Begg. "The Apostle's Prayer—Part Two" (Feb 26, 1984). https://www.truthforlife.org/resources/sermon/apostles-prayer-part-two-the/.
[124] Colossians 1:22.

understood the cross well enough to know that Jesus' sacrifice warranted a transformed life of obedience, not merely intellectual ascent to the doctrines of atonement and sanctification. He understood that sanctification meant being actually set apart from the world and truly set apart unto Christ.

My father's spiritual roots are not only in the Pentecostal movement of the early twentieth century but also the Holiness movement of the nineteenth. While he did not believe in human perfection in this life and rejected legalistic tendencies that place confidence in the flesh, he did believe that sanctification should be manifest in a visible, actual, and practical separation from the world. He did not minimize his vulnerability to temptation nor underestimate the power of his sinful nature. He knew, in the words of James, that "friendship with the world is enmity with God."[125] He took seriously the call to take up his cross daily and die to self.

In practice, this meant that there were things that our family did not watch on television, there were places we did not go for entertainment, and there were things we did not drink to relax. I never had to wonder whether my father was watching an indecent movie, sliding across the dance floor in the arms of another woman, or altered by alcohol. He was friendly toward sinners but not friendly toward the world. He held himself to a high standard of moral and ethical conduct. This was not for show. In fact, it was not what others thought that really mattered to him. It was what God thought. The measure of his spirituality was not what was seen by others but what was unseen, a life that was "holy and blameless and above reproach" in the private audience of God.[126]

In this view, there were times my father had to sacrifice the opinion of others in favor of God's opinion. During high school, he was the junior class president, a reflection of his inviting and warm personality. He was not willing, however, to compromise his

---

[125] James 4:4.
[126] Colossians 1:22.

standards, and thus excused himself from prom activities that were out of bounds. This was not easy. Nor was it easy, in the maturity of his ministry, to stand out among his peers. While at a meeting with other ministerial leaders some years ago, the ministers and their spouses attended a live show at a local theater. As the entertainment unfolded, my father felt increasingly uncomfortable. Awkward though it was before his peers, he and my mother left the theater. He did what he had to do, regardless of what others thought.

In our day, too many fathers in too many homes and too many pastors in too many churches falsely believe that Christian liberty entitles them to engage in an ever-expanding range of worldly activities. They see moral and ethical decisions in gray scale, not in black and white. They eschew legalism while promoting sensuality. This was a concern that Paul had for the church at Colossae.

It is impossible to estimate the impact that a righteous example of godliness has upon others. While my father did not do what he did to be seen by men, he was nonetheless being watched. I was watching him, and I learned what it meant to be set apart from the world, to flee temptation, to die to the flesh, and to live to Christ. And his congregation was watching also. The members of San Diego First Assembly knew that he was not merely chatter and talk about lofty spiritual ideals but an authentic example of applied and lived biblical truth. He truly believed that Jesus should be preeminent in everything.

CHAPTER 7
PREEMINENT IN HIS WORD

... if indeed you continue in the faith, stable and steadfast, not shifting from the hope of the gospel that you heard, which has been proclaimed in all creation under heaven, and of which I, Paul, became a minister.
Colossians 1:23

IN PRINCIPLE

William Tyndale (1494-1536) was an English scholar who is best known for his translation of the Bible into English. The later King James New Testament (1611) is almost exclusively (93 percent) the work of Tyndale.[127] In the King James Old Testament, most of the Pentateuch (85 percent) is attributable to Tyndale. This work was accomplished almost entirely alone, through tedious and meticulous effort and mastery of biblical languages. It was also done in the face of unending persecution from religionists in England and on the Continent who considered Tyndale's work an affront to the Catholic Church. He was opposed by kings and theologians alike. He incurred Henry VIII's wrath for his opposition to the annulment of his marriage to Anne Boleyn; he was vociferously opposed by Thomas More, a Catholic lawyer who, finding an Englishman in possession

---

[127] Melvyn Bragg. *William Tyndale: A Very Brief History* (London: The Society for Promoting Christian Knowledge, 2017), 85.

of Tyndale's Bible, personally "whipped him at a tree in his garden, called the Tree of Truth, after sent him to the Tower to be racked."[128] Thomas More found common purpose with Henry VIII in attacking Tyndale, whom he regarded as a Protestant heretic. His attacks, in the view of Tyndale's biographer, reveal "the malicious, all but insane aspect of the man who was to be made a saint."[129] In the end, Tyndale's love for the Bible would cost him his life. Betrayed by a friend, he was found guilty of heresy. He was ignominiously strangled to death while tied to a stake, his body burned after his death.

The influence of Tyndale lives on in his transformation of the English language and his influence upon the English-language view of the Bible. The King James Version, supported by Tyndale's earlier work, has sold more copies than any other book in the world. The familiar phrasing of the first chapter of Genesis ("In the beginning God created heaven and earth"), the Lord's prayer, the Beatitudes, the prologue to John's Gospel ("And the word was made flesh and dwelt among us"), and much of the New Testament owe their origins to Tyndale.

> His words, idioms, and phrases are still spoken daily and this continued use proves not only their quality but their indispensability: "see the writing on the wall"; "cast the first stone"; "the salt of the earth"; "a thorn in the flesh"; "fight the good fight"; "from strength to strength"; "the blind lead the blind"; "sick unto death"; "the powers that be".[130]

But Tyndale's greatest legacy is his to-the-death support of the Protestant doctrine of *Sola Scriptura* (by Scripture alone), which restored the Bible to its authoritative and infallible position in the

---

[128] Bragg, *William Tyndale*, 49.
[129] Bragg, *William Tyndale*, 56.
[130] Bragg, *William Tyndale*, 91.

PREEMINENT IN HIS WORD

church, in line with Luther's declaration that "the entire life and being of the church lie in the Word of God."[131]

Paul urges the Colossians to "continue in the faith, stable and steadfast, not shifting from the hope of the gospel you have heard."[132] This is the gospel of Jesus Christ, the good news of the cross, the message of redemption. It is also the panoramic witness of redemptive hope written across the span of Scripture, from Genesis to Revelation, which—along with all that is between—together comprise the Word of God. This Word, which became flesh in the person of Jesus, "has been proclaimed in all creation under heaven."

The priority of God's Word is a theme of God's Word. Psalm 119, the longest chapter in the Bible, declares the priority of God's Word as its singular subject, a Word which guides the Psalmist's every step and illuminates his path amid the surrounding darkness: "Your word is a lamp to my feet and a light to my path."[133]

God's Word is the foundation of parenting: "You shall teach them [the words of the LORD] diligently to your children, and shall talk of them when you sit in your house, and when you walk by the way, and when you lie down, and when you rise."[134]

God's Word is the guide to success in the battles of life: "This Book of the Law shall not depart from your mouth, but you shall meditate on it day and night, so that you may be careful to do according to all that is written in it. For then you will make your way prosperous, and then you will have good success."[135]

God's Word is the key to spiritual purity: "I have stored up your word in my heart, that I might not sin against you."[136]

God's Word is a spiritual weapon: "For the word of God is living and active, sharper than any two-edged sword."[137]

---

[131] James C. Wilhoit and Leland Ryken. *Effective Bible Teaching* (Grand Rapids, Michigan: Baker Academic, 2012), Kindle loc 61.
[132] Colossians 1:23.
[133] Psalm 119:105.
[134] Deuteronomy 6:7.
[135] Joshua 1:8.
[136] Psalm 119:11.

God's Word is the source of spiritual fruitfulness: "As to what is sown on good soil, this is the one who hears the word and understands it. He indeed bears fruit and yields, in one case a hundredfold, in another sixty, and in another thirty."[138]

God's Word sustains the very order of the universe: "He upholds the universe by the word of his power."[139]

And God's Word is the eternal standard against which everything has, is, or will be judged: "Heaven and earth will pass away, but my words will not pass away."[140]

It is to the task of proclaiming this Word that Paul devoted his life as "a minister." His vocation was to proclaim the Word, which he knew to be the basis of faith: "So faith comes from hearing, and hearing through the word of Christ."[141] His message was not created out of his head, derived from his extensive learning, or based upon his experiences of Jewish and Roman culture. His message was not speculative and subjective. Instead, his message was the revealed truth, conveyed to him in the Hebrew Bible (our Old Testament) and enlarged by his personal encounter with Jesus and the witness of the apostles among whom he was counted. He never deviated from the gospel message entrusted to him, warning others to ignore any and every false teacher: "But even if we or an angel from heaven should preach to you a gospel contrary to the one we preached to you, let him be accursed."[142]

Paul's warning fits with an imperative I have expressed many times to my own children and in the interest of their eternal well-being, such that they can repeat it by heart:

> No matter what the President or the Supreme Court say; no matter what the science or the culture say; no matter what your

---

[137] Hebrews 4:12.
[138] Matthew 13:23.
[139] Hebrews 1:3.
[140] Matthew 24:35.
[141] Romans 10:17.
[142] Galatians 1:8.

teachers or your classmates say; no matter what X or ChatGPT say; no matter what your pastor or your youth leader say; no matter what your grandparents or your sibling say; and *no matter what I say* ... if it in any way contradicts God's Word, if it contradicts the Bible, don't believe it!

How does one stay true to Christ? It is by hearing, understanding, and obeying his Word. The Word inspires faith, creates stability, and prevents wandering to the right or to the left. Paul understood that Jesus' preeminence in his Word is required for perseverance and endurance. If reference to his Word is lost and if sight of Jesus is obscured, faith is easily shipwrecked. But if Jesus' Word is given priority, we can confidently "continue in the faith, stable and steadfast, not shifting from the hope of the gospel."[143]

IN PRACTICE

In the early 1990s, my father took a several-month sabbatical, which was granted by San Diego First Assembly in recognition of his years of pastoral service. Of all the things he could have done during this time, he chose to attend lectures at the University of Cambridge (Cambridge, England), including those of Ernst Bammel (1923-1996). Brammel was a German Protestant theologian who completed his doctoral studies in Bonn before becoming a professor at the University of Münster in 1984.[144] He also held visiting professorships at the University of Cambridge, where he was a Reader in Jewish and Early Christian Studies. Textual criticism—"thinking critically about manuscripts and variations in the biblical texts found in those manuscripts, in order to identify the original reading of the Bible"[145]—has deep roots at Cambridge, which is

---

[143] Colossians 1:23.

[144] Ernst Brammel. https://de.wikipedia.org/wiki/Ernst_Bammel.

[145] Brandon Crowe. "Textual Criticism: What It Is and Why You Need It" (Feb 11, 2019). https://faculty.wts.edu/posts/textual-criticism-what-it-is-and-why-you-need-it/.

home to Brooke Foss Westcott (1825-1901) and Fenton John Anthony Hort (1828-1892), arguably the founders of modern textual criticism. Their Greek-language version of the New Testament (1881)—the *Westcott and Hort* (WH) text—is foundational to today's translations of the New Testament.

Textual criticism is not criticism of the inspired text of the Bible nor of the message of Scripture. Rather, it is the diligent, thoughtful, and reverent effort to provide the church—and individual believers—with the very best original text upon which to base translations. Coupled with careful work in translating the original Hebrew and Greek texts into English, students of God's Word can be confident that they hold in their hands a reliable, inerrant, inspired, and authoritative Bible. In his high regard for God's Word, my father sought to safeguard its message by using the best translation available and understanding the textual underpinnings of the Bible passages from which he read at home and preached at church. He worried about the proliferation of lower quality translations that sought to contemporize the Bible by distorting its meaning and narrowing its application. Such translations prevent the biblical text from speaking for itself and distance the reader, teacher, or pastor from its original meaning. In his personal devotions, in family altar, and in preaching, my father respected the intent of the biblical authors and appreciated the contribution of scholars like Tyndale, Westcott, and Hort, which together allow us to grasp the meaning of a Bible that expresses God's powerful and eternal Word.

My father was an expository preacher. He saw it as his duty to engage the breadth of Scripture and to uncover the meaning of specific passages of the Bible through direct interaction with the text. Just as Paul "did not shrink from declaring to you the whole counsel of God,"[146] my father faithfully and systematically moved through God's Word, verse-by-verse, chapter-by-chapter, book-by-book. He understood, in the words of A.W. Tozer, that "nothing less

---

[146] Acts 20:27.

than a whole Bible can make a whole Christian."[147] He adhered to the guidance of theologian Walter Kaiser, who advances a standard for expository, biblical preaching in line with Paul's: "It must be derived from an honest exegesis of the text, and it must constantly be kept close to the text."[148]

This exegetical approach contrasts sharply with the eisegetical approach used by many who go about imposing upon the text their own ideas rather than discovering—and submitting to—the ideas of the biblical text itself. My father understood that the only preaching that is biblical is that which preaches, exposits, and exegetes the Bible, the whole counsel of God. To do otherwise is to short-circuit the process by which the inspired Word of God transforms people's lives. When the plain meaning of Scripture is uncovered by exposition rather than concealed by layers of human ideas, it is indeed "profitable for teaching, for reproof, for correction, and for training in righteousness, that the man of God may be complete, equipped for every good work."[149] Such preaching, like the Word itself, is relevant and applicable across time and space. When our son uploaded to Apple Music sermons his grandfather had preached decades before, they struck him with an immediacy and force attributable not to the authority of a man but to the authority of the Jesus who was preeminent in his preaching of the Word.

A chief reason my father exposited God's Word each week in the pulpits of Summit Avenue and of First Assembly is that he otherwise had nothing to say. He knew people longed for an encounter with the Truth, the person of Jesus expressed in his eternal Word; no one needed his clever insights or original ideas. For him, the pulpit was not his but God's, a place for expressing God's thoughts rather than his own. The privilege of standing each week before God's people was a sacred trust and entailed accountability not to man but to God.

---

[147] A.W. Tozer. *Of God and Men: Cultivating the Divine/Human Relationship* (Chicago, Illinois: Moody Press, 2015), 67.

[148] Walter C. Kaiser, Jr. *Toward an Exegetical Theology: Biblical Exegesis for Preaching and Teaching* (Grand Rapids, Michigan: Baker Academic, 1981), Loc 162, Kindle.

[149] 2 Timothy 3:16-17.

"Not many of you should become teachers, my brothers," writes James, "for you know that we who teach will be judged with greater strictness."[150] To stray from the powerful and transformative Word of God was, for my father, a wasted opportunity and a capitulation to pride, an invitation to God's scrutiny of both.

In his view, high preaching was biblical; low preaching was not. The former proclaims God's Word with power, authority, and conviction; the latter circumvents God's Word to proclaim a human message that is weak, powerless, and unconvicting. Of the latter, there are two variations identified by Moses in his instructions to Israel: "You shall not add to the word that I command you, nor take from it, that you may keep the commandments of the LORD your God that I command you."[151] John provides a similar admonition at the conclusion of his prophetic vision:

> I warn everyone who hears the words of the prophecy of this scroll: If anyone adds anything to them, God will add to that person the plagues described in this scroll. And if anyone takes words away from this scroll of prophecy, God will take away from that person any share in the tree of life and in the Holy City, which are described in this scroll.[152]

Together, Moses and John provide bidirectional warnings against adding to or subtracting from God's commandments and prophetic words, warnings which pertain to all of Scripture but are widely ignored in our day. On the one hand, the "addition" standard is transgressed by false religionists who supplement biblical truth with extra-biblical revelations, elevating human insights and experiences to an idolatrous level. This violation is heedless of the warning of Proverbs: "Do not add to his [God's] words, lest he rebuke you and you be found a liar."[153] On the other, the "subtraction" standard is

---

[150] James 3:1.
[151] Deuteronomy 4:2.
[152] Revelation 22:18-19.

transgressed by progressive fathers and preachers who reject biblical truth claims and moral requirements to accommodate the worldview and moral relativism of the culture, directing children and congregants down a course of compromise and perdition. The consequences of both are extreme: plagues for the first, death for the second.

In my father's teaching at home and preaching at church, he avoided these perils by staying close to the Word and to its clear, accessible, and plain message. His expository approach modeled for his listeners how the Bible can be read and studied individually and devotionally. His greatest teachers were not professors at Wheaton College or Fuller Seminary but Sunday School teachers and family members, ordinary people who grasped the plain meaning of Scripture. In this, he concurs with Wheaton professors James Wilhoit and Leland Ryken, who write in their book, *Effective Bible Teaching*:

> We can celebrate the place for scholarship in understanding the Bible and at the same time announce that the central message and moral teachings of the Bible are so clear that ordinary people can discover them on their own. We have found that virtually any Bible passage contains within itself the data needed to unpack most of its meanings.[154]

My father considered the Bible an inexhaustible resource for preaching. He was skilled at breaking down a passage to uncover the depths of its meaning while understanding its context and its continuity with the broader themes of Scripture. Outside resources, when used, were secondary and supplemental, never interfering with the speaking of the Holy Spirit through his Word. By contrast, many pastors today are overly reliant upon study helps, other's sermon

---

[153] Proverbs 30:6.
[154] Wilhoit, *Effective Bible Teaching*, 7.

notes, or their own, preconceived ideas, putting these ahead of Bible engagement. Some quote extensively—without attribution—the work and ideas of others. They liberally cut and paste from Google or ChatGPT. This is not only lazy but unethical. It substitutes plagiarism for an encounter with the living Word. The feeblest effort to engage directly with God's Word is infinitely preferable to the most eloquent fabrications.

My father was once asked to speak at a conference held at his alma mater, Luther College. Since his time as a student in the 1950s, Luther—not unlike many Christian colleges and universities—had taken a decidedly progressive turn, in keeping with the descent of the Evangelical Lutheran Church in America, to which it belongs. For him, this was an opportunity to cast the light of God's Word in a place of gathering darkness. During his message, he used an illustration gleaned from Scottish preacher Ian Pitt-Watson, careful to acknowledge Pitt-Watson as its source. The story was of a young girl's doll, which had become worn and tattered by constant use. Her mother was perplexed at her daughter's attachment, until she realized that the significance of this doll derived not from its appearance but from the value attached to it by her daughter: the doll was loved. After the service concluded, my father was approached by a woman who had once heard Ian Pitt-Watson use this very illustration. "I was listening," she said, "to see if you would give him credit." My father's credibility as a father and as a pastor rested upon such attention to detail, such commitment to honesty and integrity in handling God's Word.

Above all, my father submitted to the Word of God in his conduct, not merely in his words. The Bible was the standard against which his ideas, his attitudes, his beliefs, and his behaviors were judged. He knew that he must first submit himself to its authority before asking others to do so. He had to first experience the sharp cuts of God's Word, "piercing to the division of soul and spirit, of joints and of marrow, and discerning the thoughts and intentions of the heart," before wielding the two-edge sword of God's Word in the pulpit.[155] And he understood that if he did not live according to the Word he studied at home, he had no authority in the church. And if he did not live according to the Word he preached at church, he had no authority in the home. The consistency between his expressed principles and his lived practices were the basis of his effectiveness. Without this integrity, he would not be the father and the pastor that I know, respect, and love.

In the pulpits of too many churches and in the homes of too many families, the Word of God has virtually disappeared. The authority of Scripture has been replaced by the authority of man. The gospel has been replaced by human philosophies. The worldview of the Bible has been replaced by the worldview of the culture. As a result, congregants and children are lost and confused. Hosea's warnings to wayward Israel are prescient: "My people are destroyed for lack of knowledge; because you have rejected knowledge, I reject you from being a priest to me. And since you have forgotten the law of your God, I also will forget your children."[156]

I am eternally grateful for the example of my father, my pastor. My father did not forget the law of God, the Word of God. He was faithful at home and at church to the letter and the intent of the Bible. He was faithful as a priest in the home and as a preacher in the church. He was the same man in the pulpit as he was in the parsonage. He articulated the principles of God's Word and validated them in practice through an authentic life of godliness and humility.

My father was not perfect, but he served a perfect Jesus. By making Jesus preeminent—in word and deed, in thought and action, in principle and practice—he has made a lasting, indelible, and Christ-honoring impression upon the lives of those in his family and those in his church. By putting Jesus first—in his incarnation, in his creation, in his church, in his resurrection, in his cross, in his mercy,

---

[155] Hebrews 4:12.
[156] Hosea 4:6.

in his Word—he has opened the hearts of his children and his congregants to the gospel, to biblical faith, and to everlasting life in Christ. He has truly sought to make Jesus preeminent in everything.

When one day I stand before family and friends to offer a final tribute to my father and my pastor, may I honor him and the Jesus he so deeply loved by heeding his request: *"Make sure you don't talk about how great I was but how great Jesus is."*

AFTERWORD
THE PRIORITY OF EXAMPLE

Be imitators of me, as I am of Christ.
1 Corinthians 11:1

My father attaches special significance—as do I—to the continuity of generations represented by the Canoe German Methodist Church Cemetery, more so than do either my mother or my wife, Shari. The fact that generations of the Dresselhaus family are buried in this serene corner of rural Iowa does not move them as it does my father and me. When my father informed me some years ago that a plot was available to us next to his and my mother's for a very reasonable sum of $100, I immediately—and excitedly—called Shari with the wonderful news. Her enthusiasm did not match my own.

Legacy is not about cemeteries, however, but about enduring examples. Examples set by one generation determine the behavior of the next. This cuts both ways: good examples set by one generation increase the likelihood of good behavior in the next; bad examples set by one generation increase the likelihood of bad behavior in the next. There is an important proviso: vices tend to be stickier than virtues. This is proven by every father's experience, as we observe our foibles and faults so effortlessly adopted by our children. It is the sad reality that our original sinfulness is the one attribute that is reliably transmitted from one generation to the next. It is natural to share our sinful proclivities with our children; it is a part of our spiritual DNA that passes to them as certainly as the color of our skin. What is supernatural—beyond nature—is when fathers transmit to their offspring a glorious heritage that is godly and faithful, sharing across time not the faults of the flesh but the merits of Christ.

Imitation is highest—and not mere flattery—when it is imitation of Christ. When the next generation gets a glimpse of Jesus through the words we say, the beliefs we express, and the examples we set, a profound and powerful dynamic is set in motion. Paul's life was powerful not because he was powerful but because a powerful Jesus worked through him. He boasted not in his strength but in his weakness, "so that the power of Christ may rest upon me ... For when I am weak, then I am strong."[157] This is another way of saying, in the words of John the Baptist, "He must increase, but I must decrease."[158]

The key to the spiritual legacy of fathers and of pastors is the attitude of Paul and of John the Baptist. It is the attitude expressed also by my father and my pastor, whose enduring desire was to magnify people's view of Jesus and minimize their view of himself. This requires humility and obedience. It requires death to the wants, the desires, and the needs of oneself in favor of the life of Christ within.

A magnified Jesus results when the principles of his preeminence outlined by Paul in the first chapter of Colossians are put into practice. The practice of these principles cannot be partial, for if Jesus is not preeminent in everything, he is preeminent in nothing. For fathers and pastors, we may assess the quality of our example and predict the character of our legacy by answering these seven questions:

---

[157] 2 Corinthians 12:9-10.
[158] John 3:30.

1. Is Jesus preeminent in his incarnation, in his identification with us as both the Son of God and the Son of Man?
2. Is Jesus preeminent in his creation, in the reality that the universe was spoken into existence by his powerful Word and that man is specially created in his image, not commonly descended?
3. Is Jesus preeminent in his church, in the coordinated and unified relationship of believers who comprise his body under the headship of Christ, to whom the body is completely obedient?
4. Is Jesus preeminent in his resurrection, in the glorious truth that we live because he lives?
5. Is Jesus preeminent in his cross, in the atoning fact that the death penalty owed us was taken by Christ, who alone forgives and who makes us holy and acceptable to God?
6. Is Jesus preeminent in his mercy, which has been lavished upon us so that we may show it to others?
7. Is Jesus preeminent in his Word, which is the reliable, infallible, inerrant, and eternal rule for faith and for life?

I am a work in progress. I am convicted by my father's example and drawn to the Christ he so faithfully serves. I would not be the Christian I am today were it not for the example of my father at home and my pastor at church. I recognize that many of my generation are *not* Christians today because of the example set by fathers at home and pastors at church. Before the next generation, before my son and my daughter, I aspire to emulate Christ in a manner worthy of their imitation, in keeping with the example set for me by my father, my pastor. I pray they see Jesus more than they see me, that they see his magnificence rather than my many shortcomings. There are attitudes of mind and heart that yet need to die so that Jesus may shine through me more brightly. Obeying Jesus in this way—putting the principles of his preeminence into practice—is indeed the most loving thing any father can do for his family or any pastor for his church.

The example I set—that you set—matters not just for time but for eternity. The only thing that matters for my posterity—and yours—is that they spend eternity in heaven and not in hell. With this in view, I pray you will join me, both at home and at church, in the priority of making Jesus first and foremost, so that in everything he might be preeminent.

EPILOGUE

On a brisk December evening in 2023, the Dresselhaus family assembled at my sister Ann's home in Happy's Inn, Montana, our collective presence raising this small town's population of 78 by 14 percent. We did so to celebrate the completion of Ann's vacation home, built as a gathering place for family in the pristine tranquility of a remote forest. And we did so to celebrate the day over two thousand years ago when Jesus, the incarnate Son of God, entered our experience as a helpless baby in an equally inconspicuous place called Bethlehem.

We read the story of Christmas from Luke's Gospel and then exchanged gifts before the warm glow of the fireplace. After the excitement had died down, I surprised my father with a gift conceived years before and completed in the months preceding: a prepublication copy of *The Preeminent Jesus in My Father, My Pastor*. I explained its origin and purpose by reading from the Introduction, recalling a day eight years prior when my father instructed me to honor his memory with this imperative: *"Make sure you don't talk about how great I was but how great Jesus is."*

I do not remember what words of appreciation were said in response. Seared instead in my mind is a picture of my father—then eighty-eight years old—seated on the hearth of the fireplace, head bowed and eyes moistened with tears. What was he thinking? Why was he crying?

Though at home and at church my father was always sensitive and caring, he typically did not reveal his emotions with tears, even if profoundly moved. In this instance, however, tears betrayed a response from deep within, a place beyond words. Though the assessment that follows is speculative, I believe it is true, derived from many years of observing my father and my pastor in his principles and in his practices.

First and foremost, my father was overwhelmed with gratitude to Jesus, who died for his sins on the cross, raised him to new life through his powerful resurrection, and intercedes for him in eternal glory at the Father's right hand. This Jesus has the unrivaled place of priority in my father's family life and my pastor's church life.

In the moment, my father may have recalled the boyhood decision to follow Christ, kneeling with his mother in their farmhouse kitchen. He may have remembered times spent at the altar of the little Pentecostal church on the wrong side of the railroad tracks. He may have thought of the call of the Holy Spirit—through the encouraging words of his father one day while working together in the barn—to pursue a life of pastoral ministry. Perhaps he remembered the aspiration of a young pastor written on a birthday cake a half century prior: "that in everything he might be preeminent." In a moment, memories may have flashed across his mind of solitude with God in prayer and in the study of his Word, private times that drew him closer to his Savior and prepared him to serve his family and his congregation.

His tears certainly flowed from thoughts of his family. He may have remembered his paternal grandmother, Emma Dresselhaus, who set the spiritual direction of our family, or of his godly parents, Elmer and Gladys, who set a profound yet practical example of godliness in their daily lives on a dairy farm in rural Iowa. He was thinking of family gathered with him that night in Montana: his lifelong helpmate, his two children, a daughter-in-law, three grandchildren, a grandson-in-law, and two great grandchildren. Most of all, he was grateful for family who had in the past and are in the present putting Jesus first. If spiritual reproduction across generations is the final measure of spiritual fruitfulness, then perhaps this book was a heavenly signal to my father of a job well done.

Without question, my father's tears also flowed from an abiding appreciation of the many people who have ministered to him and the many people to whom he has had the privilege of ministering. His love for the church is expansive and undiminished, encompassing congregants who nurtured his young faith at Decorah Assembly of God, gave him his first opportunities as an associate and then senior pastor at Summit Avenue Assembly of God, and invited him to lead San Diego First Assembly for thirty-three years. This love is specific for countless individuals who taught him, encouraged him, prayed for him, corrected him, supported him, and shared his desire to make Jesus first as head over his church.

It may be that tears are a specific reflection of the image of God stamped upon our nature. Of all the creatures in God's creation, only people share this capacity—animals do not. We know that Jesus shed tears, and he did so in his humanity as the Son of Man and in his divinity as the Son of God. What moved Jesus to tears was what mattered most, what mattered ultimately, what mattered eternally—the eternal souls whom he loved and for whom he would die.

On that serene Christmas night in the remote wilderness of Montana, the tears shed in time may have flowed also from eternity, if only because my father, my pastor has loved and lived so "that in everything he might be preeminent."

QUESTIONS FOR REFLECTION & DISCUSSION

INTRODUCTION

1. What are the immediate and eternal implications of granting—or not granting—Jesus his rightful place of preeminence?

2. Why is it important that the next generation see Jesus through the godly examples of fathers and pastors?

3. How is leadership in the home connected to leadership in the church?

4. How has demotion of Jesus to a position of secondary importance contributed to the decline of the Christian family and the Christian church in our country?

5. Why is obeying Jesus the most loving thing any father can do for his family or any pastor for his church?

CHAPTER 1 – PREEMINENT IN HIS INCARNATION

1. How do the divine and the human come together in the incarnate Jesus?

2. Why is the incarnation both marvelous and mysterious?

3. What are the dangers of emphasizing Jesus' humanity over his divinity or his divinity over his humanity?

4. Of what did Jesus empty himself during his time on earth? Of what did he *not* empty himself?

5. How did Jesus' lifestyle, manner of teaching, and use of illustrations align with his incarnate nature?

CHAPTER 2 – PREEMINENT IN HIS CREATION

1. In what ways is Genesis the foundation of the biblical worldview upon which Paul builds in his letter to the Colossians?

2. What was Jesus' role in the creation of the universe and the creation of man?

3. How is Jesus' preeminence in creation linked to his preeminence in salvation?

4. Why is Jesus' preeminence the central issue in the battle of worldviews in our day?

5. Is there evidence in support of the thesis that if Jesus is not preeminent in everything, he will soon be preeminent in nothing?

CHAPTER 3 – PREEMINENT IN HIS CHURCH

1. Why is the head-body relationship a compelling metaphor for the spiritual relationship of Christ to his church?

QUESTIONS FOR REFLECTION & DISCUSSION

2. What light does this metaphor shed on the priority of obedience in the relationship of the body of Christ to its head? On the dependence of the body upon the head?

3. What are the boundaries of Christian freedom?

4. What is the spiritual prognosis of a believer who willingly separates from the body of Christ?

5. With which family do you primarily identify: your biological family or your spiritual family?

CHAPTER 4 – PREEMINENT IN HIS RESURRECTION

1. Why are Jesus' death and resurrection the twin pillars of the Christian faith? What are the consequences if the latter is not true?

2. What does Paul mean when he describes Jesus as "the firstborn from the dead" (Colossians 1:18)? How does this mirror his earlier statement that Jesus is "the firstborn of all creation" (Colossians 1:15)?

3. How does Jesus' resurrection resolve doubts of his Word and distrust of his promises?

4. What is meant by the saying: "Tradition is the living faith of the dead; traditionalism is the dead faith of the living"?

5. In view of the brevity of life and the expanse of eternity, how should success in this life be measured or our influence upon the next generation judged?

CHAPTER 5 – PREEMINENT IN HIS CROSS

1. On what basis is a person justified (made righteous) before God? Why did Paul say, "But far be it from me to boast except in the cross of our Lord Jesus Christ"?

2. What is the role of the cross in drawing people to Jesus?

3. Is the disappearance of the cross from many churches and sanctuaries of any significance?

4. How does the story of Abraham's sacrifice of Isaac help us understand John 3:16?

5. If Jesus' death spares us from the wrath of God, what is in store for those outside of the forgiveness of the cross?

CHAPTER 6 – PREEMINENT IN HIS MERCY

1. What is man's original nature and his natural disposition toward God?

2. Why did God seek reconciliation with people who are both evil in behavior and hostile in attitude?

3. How are mercy and justice brought together at Jesus' crucifixion?

4. Why did Corrie Ten Boom, upon forgiving her former captor, state, "I had never known God's love so intensely as I did then"?

QUESTIONS FOR REFLECTION & DISCUSSION

5. How should we live if the purpose of the reconciliation accomplished on the cross is "to present you holy and blameless and above reproach before him" (Colossians 1:22)?

CHAPTER 7 – PREEMINENT IN HIS WORD

1. Does your church conform to Luther's belief that "the entire life and being of the church lie in the Word of God"?

2. What is the role of God's Word in making sure that believers "continue in the faith, stable and steadfast" (Colossians 1:23)?

3. Why is textual criticism important to the church and to those who value the accuracy and reliability of the Bible?

4. What is the difference between exegesis and eisegesis? Which is the preferred approach in the teaching God's Word in corporate and small-group settings?

5. Is it ethical to incorporate into one's sermons or teachings the ideas of others without attribution?

AFTERWORD – THE PRIORITY OF EXAMPLE

1. What is the legacy that you are passing on to your children at home or to the next generation at church?

2. What kind of example are you setting for your children? For the next generation?

3. In your relationship to Jesus, do you believe, in practice, that "he must increase, but I must decrease" (John 3:30) or that "I must increase, but he must decrease"?

4. Who in your life best exemplifies the practice of Jesus' preeminence?

5. Is Jesus first and foremost in your life, so "that in everything he might be preeminent" (Colossians 1:18)?

ACKNOWLEDGMENTS

While this book focuses on the work of Jesus in and through the life and ministry of my father and my pastor, it is impossible to think of him—both in the home and in the church—apart from my mother, Elnora. They were devoted and inseparable partners in parenting and in ministry.

My mother is recognized as a talented musician, facile at both piano and organ. Few can match her ability to improvise almost any hymn or chorus in any key at any time. She was the motive force behind my sister and me studying violin, sharing her love of music and accompanying us as our outstanding pianist. The three of us often performed together over the years. My father's lesser musical abilities excluded him from the family ensemble.

My mother set an example of hard work and discipline, of deep integrity and spiritual devotion. She was as involved in the ministries of the local church as my father was. My mother and father were one in purpose and one in mind. They were united in their love for God, in love for one another, in love for their children, and in love for God's people. I could just as easily have written a volume celebrating the preeminent Jesus in my mother. My debt to her is no less than my debt to my father. Both are beyond my ability to repay.

Were it not for the encouragement and support of Robert Menzies, a New Testament scholar, author, missionary, and friend, I would not have written my first book, *Seven Deadly Lies in the Culture and the Church*, nor this book. He was a mentor through the process of conceptualizing, writing, and ultimately publishing *Seven Deadly Lies*, which paved the way for this book. However, I do not share with him responsibility for any deficiencies in this or my prior manuscript; such belongs solely to me.

Grant Hochman reviewed the manuscript and detected important opportunities to correct and improve it. His meticulous attention to detail contributed in many ways to its final form.

I am indebted to my wife Shari, who encouraged and supported me through the process of writing this book, offering valuable input that improved the manuscript in countless instances. She is the love of my life and my best friend. As a couple, we are doubly blessed by—and doubly accountable for—the spiritual heritage of both of our fathers. Her grandfather, Ewalt Bartel, and father, LeRoy Bartel, have passed to us a legacy of devotion and honor to Christ, both in principle and in practice. Our two families could not be more similar in the only regard that matters: the preeminence of Jesus. Shari and I desire that our children will continue in the path charted for them by God's Word and walked in by their grandparents. We hope they will look beyond our imperfections to see the perfect Jesus that we love and serve. Our priority prayer for our son, Noah, our daughter, Emma, and our posterity is that Jesus will be preeminent in everything.

ABOUT THE AUTHOR

Dr. Timothy Dresselhaus is Clinical Professor Emeritus, School of Medicine, University of California, San Diego. He received his bachelor's degree in history from the University of California, San Diego, graduating Summa cum Laude and Phi Beta Kappa, while also winning the Armand Rappaport prize, the History Department's highest honor, for his thesis on Arthur Schopenhauer, the intellectual forerunner to Friedrich Nietzsche. He received his medical degree from the University of California, San Francisco and was elected to the Alpha Omega Alpha national medical honor society. He completed his Internal Medicine residency at the University of California, San Diego, serving an additional year as a Chief Medical Resident before joining its faculty. He earned a Masters in Public Health from the University of Washington, Seattle. His professional career has encompassed healthcare administration, health services research, and medical education. He served as Chief of Primary Care at the VA San Diego Healthcare System and in national leadership roles for the Veterans Health Administration, Washington, DC. Author or co-author of thirty-five research articles, he has been a Principal Investigator, Co-Principal Investigator, or Co-Investigator on multiple funded research projects. He has served as a teacher, elder, and musician in his local church and in national leadership roles related to world missions, as a university trustee, and as the author of Christian position papers related to medical ethics and biblical creation. In 2023, he published *Seven Deadly Lives in the Culture and the Church*. He lives with his wife, Shari, and their son and daughter in San Diego, California.

NOW AVAILABLE ON amazon

A campaign of deception originating in Eden threatens the church and the next generation. Drawing upon a career in the academy, Dresselhaus traces the spread of seven deadly lies—all rooted in a false, materialist worldview—from campus culture to the pulpits and pews of the church. He challenges leaders, pastors, parents, and students to enjoin the battle for minds and hearts by raising the standard of God's Word.

"A significant book in the mold of Francis Schaeffer's *A Christian Manifesto*."

Robert P. Menzies, PhD - Author of *Christ-Centered* and *The End of History*

"A must-read for pastors, teachers, and faith leaders in response to the lies of a woke generation."

Jim Johnson, EdD - Professor Emeritus, Point Loma Nazarene University

"Should be on the reading list of every Christian leader and college-age student."

Kermit S. Bridges, DMin - President, Southwestern Assemblies of God University

www.ingramcontent.com/pod-product-compliance
Lightning Source LLC
Chambersburg PA
CBHW032038040426
42449CB00007B/938